CONSTRUCTING WORLDS OTHERWISE

Societies in Movement and Anticolonial Paths in Latin America

"A survey of sustained autonomous people's movements in Latin America that helps us rethink survival in the context of the extractivist State. It reimagines change even as it raises the quintessential question of how to move from episodic to radical social transformation."
—Johanna Fernández, historian and author of *The Young Lords: A Radical History*

"This is a book that follows the lead of Latin America's societies in movement, from below and to the left. Zibechi takes us to the streets in these pages, helping us think through and work beyond the world's crises with solutions and theories made by movements themselves. It is essential reading for expanding the radical imagination."
—Benjamin Dangl, author of *The Five Hundred Year Rebellion: Indigenous Movements and the Decolonization of History in Bolivia*

"Raul has gifted us with a powerful tool for understanding pueblos / societies in movement—helping us to better understand what they are interrupting historically and breaking from theoretically—all grounded in movement practice-based theories. This is an absolute must read for everyone wanting to understand our world(s) and how they are already being changed, horizontally and affectively."
—Marina Sitrin, author of *Everyday Revolutions: Horizontalism and Autonomy in Argentina*

CONSTRUCTING WORLDS OTHERWISE

Societies in Movement and Anticolonial Paths in Latin America

Raúl Zibechi

Translated by George Ygarza Quispe

Constructing Worlds Otherwise: Societies in Movement and Anticolonial Paths in Latin America

© 2024 Raúl Zibechi
This edition © AK Press
ISBN: 978-1-84935-542-1
E-ISBN: 978-1-84935-543-8
Library of Congress Control Number: 2023948708

AK Press
370 Ryan Ave. #100
Chico, CA 95973
www.akpress.org
akpress@akpress.org

AK Press
33 Tower St.
Edinburgh EH6 7BN
Scotland
www.akuk.com
ak@akedin.demon.co.uk

The above addresses would be delighted to provide you with the latest AK Press distribution catalog, which features books, pamphlets, zines, and stylish apparel published and/or distributed by AK Press. Alternatively, visit our websites for the complete catalog, latest news, and secure ordering.

Cover illustration by Pilar Emitxin
Cover design by John Yates | www.stealworks.com
Printed in the USA on acid-free, recycled paper

Contents

Translator's Note

"This is not Latin America."

That was the retort one of my colleagues gave in response to our discussion of how best to organize the student body. It was our first collective meeting in support of a compañera who was unable to secure enough funding from our academic institution to support them in their graduate studies program. Prior to this meeting, we had shared stories and examples from other parts of the country and the world on how best to confront the exploitative power of the neoliberal institution. Some of us brought up examples from South Africa and Chile, regions of the world where students had recently occupied administrative spaces and subverted the hierarchies that upheld structures of power in higher education. We mentioned the #FeesMustFall movement of South Africa, where students had taken over administrative halls and established popular assemblies in a months-long struggle to fight fee increases at University of Witwatersrand, a movement that quickly spread to other campuses across South Africa. We talked about Chile in 2011, where a highly selective voucher program placed higher education out of reach for many working-class students. That year, student protests led to what came to be known as the long Chilean winter, during which students at all levels of schooling confronted the privatized education system. At the time, Chilean students made connections with

1

the historical struggles of the Mapuche, the Indigenous peoples of Wallmapu, what is today commonly known as Chile.

However, what had initially started with support from the entire graduate student body in our department, ultimately dwindled to a handful of us.

While the reactionary quip, "this is not Latin America," may seem like an apropos announcement given the meek mobilizations in the US in contrast to other places, it stands in sharp contrast with the resounding calls of solidarity from yesteryear. In the mid- to late-twentieth century, groups like the American Indian Movement, the Young Lords, and others read their local struggles alongside the fight against occupations, dispossession, and imperialism abroad. Not to mention, campuses across the US were forming strong bonds with movements across the world, such as the Third World Liberation Front at San Francisco State University. A former college organizer himself, it was Stokely Carmichael whose resounding 1967 call for Black Power, made the analogy between Black subjugation in the urban ghettos and colonialism abroad. Noting the ghetto's "colonial patterns," Carmichael and his coauthor Charles V. Hamilton described the politics of Blackness as one predicated on communality, arguing that capitalism stood in contrast to these formations as it reinforced racial hierarchies because it was rooted in the subjugation of poor folks in a manner not unlike the colonies abroad. Yet, since then, the most visible movements for social change in the United States, including those on campuses, have seemingly interpellated Fukuyama's dictum of the end of history.[1]

---

1.   An American political scientist, Francis Fukuyama had by the end of the Cold War captured the sentiments of the neoconservative class by declaring that the fall of Communism seemingly brought a close to humanity's search for a sociopolitical pax. In his book, *The End of History and the Last Man*, he argues Western liberal democracies were in themselves the final historical epoch.

What happened?

The statement "this is not Latin America," can be interpreted as a projection of the training received in the very institution we were looking to change. The pushback and paternalistic response we received from some of our "colleagues" in our attempts to connect with struggles abroad reflected many of the characteristics of Area Studies. Referring to the interdisciplinary field of research that folds diverse knowledge systems into particular geographical and cultural regions, Area Studies emerged in the post-WWII period and rose concurrently with the counterinsurgent movement that took place in the US. Just like the disciplinary field of Area Studies, it seems like the left, broadly defined, has similarly come to compartmentalize and provincialize the understanding of struggles abroad. Trading a long legacy of solidarity for Fukuyama's dictum that we are at the end of history, it seems as if the pessimism of the intellect has bled into the will of the people.

The closest revival of internationalism, like the one seen in the 1960s, would not take place until the 2008 financial crisis, when many of us here in the US were looking for models of alternative political practices to escape crisis and reimagine another world. We became inspired, for example, by the *tomas* of occupied factories in Argentina just a few years earlier. The Occupy movement began with the renaming of Freedom Square in New York and became part of the cartography of resistance along with the uprisings in Tahrir, Gaza, Greece, Spain, Brazil, and other places across the globe.

Spending time in these encampments, I was introduced to a myriad of ideas, new concepts, and social structures through the various colloquies and teach-ins that had formed. Concepts like *horizontality* and *decentralized assemblies* provided us with a new repertoire to reframe and reimagine our own organizing strategies. Occupy became a space for us to recover some of the lost

3

assemblages and networks of the past as we learned from the shared struggles of movements abroad.

One of the best reporters of such movements is Raúl Zibechi. Those of us who read Spanish or have managed to get our hands on his few texts that have been translated into English, have found an astute interlocutor between theory and practice. Accompanying various societies in movement across the southern continent, Zibechi is less an academic and more a fellow traveler, learning from communities that are constructing worlds beneath and against Latin American modernity.

In addition to rejecting the commitments to academic professionalism, Zibechi rejects the conformity that established political institutions call for. This allows Zibechi to recognize through his travels that the revolutionary path is much less linear than the traditional left has made it out to be. What Zibechi reminds us of is that, despite being in a post-Marxist epoch, we have nonetheless retained many of its dialectical frameworks, even after these frameworks were already being questioned by thinkers like Walter Benjamin.

Today, while much of the left, broadly defined, remains committed to state-centric frameworks and approaches, the most dynamic movements in Latin America have drawn upon ancestral knowledges and place-based politics to imagine worlds otherwise. This was a reality the proto-Zapatista movement was embarrassingly confronted with early on in their uprising when seeking out recruits deep in the jungles of Chiapas.

Zibechi's work forces us to question the frameworks that we—here referring to those concerned with the construction of other worlds—have taken too seriously, as well as the sociological terms used for understanding struggle and resistance. One of these notions is that of understanding change as occurring in totality. To collapse the history of resistance in the United States as part of a totality is to absolve power and reduce it to an incidental, something Zibechi vividly describes at various points throughout the text that follows. Emphasizing a totality is to ignore the fact that the dehumanization of Black life and the dispossession of Indigenous peoples were interrelated mechanisms of statecraft on which the United States was founded. Totality also works to presume that the only modes of resistance in the US are centered on civil rights, appeals to the State, and in its most radical instance, the acquisition of power itself. Totality was one of the fatal flaws I found in the Occupy movement, as it failed to understand and grasp its internal particularities, ultimately giving way to its contradictions.

The concept of societies or *pueblos* in movement, which Zibechi is most known for, breaks the stranglehold that the idea of totality has on our understanding of what resistance is and how change occurs. To understand society in the plural reverts our gaze to the *otherwise*. It takes seriously the subversive and alternative formulations we have long missed or overlooked. At the same time, it helps us to reconstruct new bridges while reassembling the networks required to create worlds otherwise.

George Ygarza Quispe
Paterson, February 2023

Preface to the English Edition

The 1960s were prodigious for antisystemic movements and struggles for collective emancipation. Among the many virtues of this period, I would like to recall that it allowed us to better understand the struggles of the peoples of the world with much greater precision than what happened in the years before and since. More than any other, it was during this period that we were able to feel the violence and pain of peoples in other parts of the world as Che Guevara proclaimed in his passionate interventions.

During this time, it was not necessary to build bridges between the struggles of the North and the South, because common sense said that we suffered for the same reasons, closely linking imperialism with capitalism. The roots of the liberatory struggles of colonized countries, of people who suffered because of their skin color and of those who lived tormented by patriarchy and machismo, converged into a single torrent of indignation bell hooks would later formulate.

I would be remiss if I did not mention that in my small town of Montevideo in Uruguay, the main left-wing newspaper, *Marcha*, led by Eduardo Galeano, would send us a monthly compilation of documents from the different movements from around the world. When we received a notebook entitled "Black Power," our hearts jumped with enthusiasm to learn about the powerful and revealing anticapitalist experiences of the Black social movement of that time in the US such as the Black Panther Party.

It is not difficult to imagine that many young Americans would have also jumped upon receiving news of the resistances of Cuba or Vietnam, that upon hearing about the Tet Offensive in 1969, had similar enthusiasm with which they attended the March on Washington and listened to Martin Luther King's famous speech on August 28, 1963. The condemnation by Martin Luther King and others of the United States's treatment of Black people resonated around the planet and was understood as something of its own by millions of people who were not African American but felt similar pains.

We called it internationalism, but it was just the common sense of the time for those of us who felt that the world was an unfair place and needed to change. We said "revolution" without imagining that soon this word would be demonized, becoming synonymous with terrorism thanks to the counterinsurgent role that the monopolized media began to play. But in those times, we were happy celebrating every victory of antisystemic struggles taking place in every corner of the planet.

Then came the terrible years of the conservative counter-revolution and we all retreated, pushed further down by conservative policies that threatened dissent everywhere.

For Latin America these were dark times, years of repression in which a few former rebels even joined the systems they once opposed, most often in high positions in companies or the State. But most of those who were with us turned inward to satisfy their own individual desires, not caring too much about the rest of humanity. This did not happen in just one country or on one single continent, but everywhere, as globalization has shown us that the whole planet is impacted in very similar ways.

Out of this darkness came January 1, 1994, which, at least for those of us in Latin America, was a light of hope, rebellion, and love that made our dreams come true. Thirty years have now passed and many of us still feel the same emotions from that early morning of the new year, when we saw thousands of Indigenous people with their faces covered occupying cities in southern Mexico.

I know that in the United States many people felt similarly. In May, I was able to attend the El Sur Resiste caravan, organized by the National Indigenous Congress. The caravan began in Chiapas and toured seven states in support of resistance against megaprojects, and I was not surprised to find a large delegation from California. The Zapatista struggle has awakened the dormant internationalism.

In the same way, in this part of the world we celebrate the Sioux resistance to the construction of the pipeline in Standing Rock and the broad alliance between native peoples of the United States, as well as the solidarity that it inspired, bringing together religious figures, Vietnam veterans, ecologists, and various social movements. We also celebrate the numerous mobilizations of Black people including Black Lives Matter and the Movement for Black Lives, struggles articulated in the streets responding to police abuses.

I also resonate with struggles like the Capitol Hill Autonomous Zone that found itself in dialogue with the Commune of Oaxaca (2006), given that they opened urban spaces as a way to find other ways of living, even for only a brief time. I am also able to recognize the way in which Cooperation Jackson is in dialogue with the network of cooperatives of CECOSESOLA, the solidarity association of cooperatives in Venezuela. Beyond the details about the way they operate, and the number of people involved, both register strong anticapitalist approaches.

We are learning that in this system there are no definitive victories, because the thousands of tentacles of the "Capitalist Hydra" (as the Zapatistas call it) attack in every imaginable place. After Standing Rock, this system has now set its sights on Canada, with the attempt to build the Coastal GasLink pipeline on the land of the Wet'suwet'en people. The Capitalist Hydra does not rest.

We have also learned that structural and monocultural projects are part of the system, exceeding the will of a government because large corporations accumulate capital by destroying people and nature without the slightest shame. These initiatives are part of a structural feature of capitalism today: accumulation by dispossession, a concept formulated by the geographer David Harvey. The only difference is that in the territories of the pueblos this accumulation takes the form of a war of dispossession, because this system militarily invades our territories to impose its projects.

Another lesson we learned is that violence against the Black population and against the Indigenous peoples of Latin America is exactly the same, because it pursues the same objectives with similar structural characteristics. Let me explain: for the elites, we the poor pueblos are merely a "surplus population," we do not serve them even for exploitation, as they no longer need us as workers or even as servants. That is why we are seeing health care systems and public education continue to worsen.

Faced with this reality, we need to build our own worlds like the Black Panthers did in the past and as the Zapatistas are doing today. Committed to the survival of Black peoples, the Panthers set up community and social programs that were, by 1969, part of their main organizing structure. From free breakfast programs and education programs for children, to community health clinics where diseases such as tuberculosis were treated. As a whole, these organizing structures comprised what could be seen as a different society, in the same way the original and Black peoples in Latin America are building today.

Given the almost permanent mobilization of sectors of the Black population in the United States, it is easy for me to find resonance with my conceptualization of "people on the move" or "societies in movement." In the US, the term "peoples," which I find to be the best translation of the commonly used Latin American term pueblo, has fallen out of fashion within the broader left. Yet, when we take the context and the historic moment of resistance into account, it seems to still be the most fitting. In the 1960s, *pueblos en movimientos*, or peoples on the move, was undoubtedly appropriate, not least because it was a sector of society that mobilized organically while building social relations different from the hegemonic ones, as can be seen from the aforementioned social programs. But societies in movement are not a permanent establishment, simply because state repression and persecution have set it back both in its organization and consciousness.

However, there are other similarities here with Latin American struggles. When we hear Malcolm X demand that his people not consume tobacco or alcohol, it reminds us of the decision of the Zapatista women to ban drinking in their own communities to prevent men from beating them or weakening the organization.

When I observe the Zapatistas during their encounters of "women who struggle," I cannot help but recall the statement put out by the Combahee River Collective in the 1970s announcing the emergence of a new feminism from below. There is an implicit dialogue between the feminism of Black lesbian women and that of the Mayan Zapatistas, which speaks to us of the overlapping oppression of class, race, and gender, something invisible to white academic women.

Yesterday and today, and always, the struggles of peoples are interwoven, linked together under the line of visibility, to the point that some inspire others, and they learn from them, overcoming distances and the most diverse geographies. The most remarkable thing, however, is that, to weave these links neither parties nor leaders, nor large organizational apparatuses are necessary, because relations are forged by the common sense of the peoples

Introduction

Those of us who are part of the anticapitalist camp are caught in the following paradox: while we have come to accept that the world has changed and that our attempts at seizing power have failed, our critical thinking has remained committed to the concepts and proposals born in another historical period, one that stretches even further back than the outbreak of the socialist camp.

This gap between the real world and our theoretical and political choices is possibly the most important source of the frustrations and weaknesses we face. In fact, we remain attached to an idea of revolution centered on the capture of state power, on the construction of hierarchical parties and organizations, as well as the planning of the steps to be taken (both strategic and tactical) set out by a small group of enlightened white males, and finally the separation of ethics from the political in order to give priority to ends over means—all of which fetishizes public action over internal growth.

A good part of the ideas that continue to shape our anti-systemic practices have turned into bars that enclose struggle in a political and conceptual prison, preventing the deployment of emancipatory energies. The centrality of the struggle for power, for example, assumes that all mobilizations and struggles must head toward that direction, subordinating concrete struggles to this "final" goal. The very concept of "final struggle," as the lyrics of "The Internationale" say, cannot but be linked to the seizure of power, is perhaps the most eternal and least creative web of ideas that can be imagined.

The question that assails us is thus: why have the people willing to give their lives for a cause found so much difficulty in questioning certainties rather than questioning life? It seems to be that there is no single reason for this behavior, since the effort to continue on the path of the old politic is a response to the conceptual as much as the psychological limitations, given that questioning certainties implies entering a field of personal insecurity.

This personal insecurity is due to the ensuing restlessness and anguish produced by the lack of forceful responses to complex situations, such as those that we find ourselves in today. Perhaps it is for this reason that our own failures and mistakes tend to hide themselves as we continue to simply place blame on imperialism and the right for all our problems, absolving us from the necessary self-criticism in order to modify our course.

As an invitation to collective dialogue and reflection, I would like to put forth a half dozen difficulties or challenges standing in the way of our critical thinking. My hope is that by articulating these impediments we may be encouraged to take up rebellious experimentation along less traveled paths, leaving behind the well-trodden path of mobilizing workers to achieve power by any means.

The first challenge can be found in the attachment to certainties, which allow us to believe, as Cornelius Castoriadis has argued in his analysis, in Marxism as a doctrine. Castoriadis has shown his ability to sustain a critical and dynamic struggle over a long time and under very adverse circumstances. This doctrine, which claims to be Marxist, has been formed by defining as an economic science, a rationalist metaphysical understanding of history that is concretized in the famous "laws of history," which endorse both the "inevitable" proletarian triumph and the millenary "hope of a guaranteed salvation."[1]

Focusing the analysis on the anticapitalist subject, the working class, the Greek French philosopher reminds us of its autodidactic history, it "constituted itself and became literate and was formed by itself," giving life to the individuals who put trust in their own strength, thought for themselves, studied under the glow of candles after strenuous fourteen hour days, and never abandoned critical reflection. When doctrinaire Marxism monopolized the workers movements, according to Castoriadis, its devastating effects became apparent: "Marxism replaced this individual with the militant activist who is indoctrinated in a Gospel; who believes in the organization, in the theory and in the bosses who possess this theory and interpret it; who tends to obey them unconditionally; who identifies with them and who is capable, most of the time, of breaking with this identification only by him/herself collapsing."[2]

Some of these certainties permeated the imaginary of the left with such intensity that they managed to defy the passage of time as well as the geographical realities and the obvious failures of its cognate revolutions. At the same time that it became installed with dogmas, these certainties ultimately nullified the possibility of self-critical reflection. The attachment to a simplified theory of a natural evolutionary order, the requirement of leaders in whom to place almost absolute trust, the centrality of the economy to explain any social process and a concept of revolution focused on the construction of a centralized power—ideas that remain valid both in the forces that bet on the seizure of power and in those that chose to embed themselves in the institutionality of electoral politics.

1.   Cornelius Castoriadis, "The Pulverization of Marxism-Leninism.," *Salmagundi* 88/89 (Fall 1990–Winter 1991): 373, 376, 377.
2.   Castoriadis, "The Pulverization of Marxism-Leninism," 378.

Much of this imaginary comes from cultures that came long before the socialist one and are actually a realignment with millenarian traditions of humanity updated by a capitalist imaginary with a scientific quality. As the Spaniard Eugenio del Río argues, socialist thought has "multi-secular roots," ranging from the Renaissance and Reformation to Christianity, being "a link in the chain of modernity."[3] It is possible, however, that the most damaging legacy of Marxism is its blind trust in progress, as Benjamin sharply emphasizes while simultaneously denouncing the same conformism of the left: "Nothing has corrupted the German working class so much as the notion that it was moving with the current."[4]

In fact, it was social democracy during its first three decades of the twentieth century that was creating a school that bet everything on technical and scientific development, considering factory work as a part of the materialization of that development—a political action in itself: "This training made the working class forget both its hatred and its spirit of sacrifice, for both are nourished by the image of enslaved ancestors rather than that of liberated grandchildren."[5]

This reflects a sense of moral superiority held by many of these militants where they believe themselves to be part of a class that will ultimately triumph as they come to possess an infallible doctrine. It is entirely true then that, as Castoriadis points out, getting rid of such a set of certainties has thus far been extremely difficult, largely because questioning this doctrine engenders a kind of vertigo as it essentially questions one's identity and the meaning of the lives that have been carved around it.

3. Eugenio del Río, *La Sombra de Marx: Estudio Crítico Sobre La Fundación Del Marxismo (1877–1900)* (Madrid: Talasa, 1993), 334.

4. Walter Benjamin, "Theses on the Philosophy of History," in *Critical Theory and Society: A Reader*, eds. Stephen Bronner and Douglas Kellner (London: Routledge, 2020), 259.

5. Benjamin, "Theses on the Philosophy of History," 260.

The second difficulty lies in the inherent problems that rest in the conversion of theory—by definition unfinished and approximate—into a doctrine with absolute certainties. It is one of the themes developed by Black feminist bell hooks in her extensive polemic with white academic feminism, which for these similar reasons remained hegemonic for quite a long time.

hooks argued that "the exclusionary practices of women who dominate the feminist discourse have made it practically impossible for new and varied theories to emerge."[6] Therefore, it was the existence of a single legitimate discourse that stifled the diversity of voices and prevented women from the grassroots from joining the movement, converting feminism into a bourgeois ideology as a result.

Consider that the tendency to dogmatism nullified the lived experiences that produced feminist theory in the first place, pretending to place itself above the feelings of the oppressed, discarding affect to prioritize a supposed scientific character. hooks goes on to cite the essay "The Way of All Ideology," by feminist philosopher Susan Griffin, who believes that "when a theory is transformed into an ideology, it begins to destroy the self and self-knowledge," attributes "the" truth and aims to "discipline real people" behind those who hold the knowledge/power.[7] "Everything that he fails to explain becomes his enemy," Griffin says in a phrase that connects us to much of our experience in the debate with the old political culture.[8]

Drawing from the debates that hooks's polemic raises, I am interested in highlighting how the conversion of ideas and theories into ideology serves the interests of a privileged social layer that

---

6.   bell hooks, *Feminist Theory: From Margin to Center* (New York: Routledge, 2015), 9.
7.   hooks, *Feminist Theory*, 10.
8.   hooks, *Feminist Theory*, 10.

dominates and legitimizing discourse, all the while perpetuating and extending its privileges, as it comes to exclude and marginalize those who may threaten them. Those who question this discourse are demonized because they would be questioning privileges within the emancipatory camp, be they white feminists, political and trade union leaders, or revolutionaries from dependent countries trained in universities.

These ideological formations are ultimately removed from the ways that oppressed peoples and social groups express themselves, those whom these ideologies proclaim to speak for. The elite class who holds the heritage of critical thinking, are inherently conservative, having much to lose, including their status, comforts, and the recognition that provides them with an unbearable feeling of superiority. That is why they cling to a doctrinal practice far removed from reality, taking hostage the ideas and thoughts from below, a space that these elites prefer never to step into again, if they ever did.

The third difficulty is trying to differentiate between groups opposing systemic structures and the system itself as they both seem to operate under similar structures. I bring in here the wise words of Fernand Braudel when he reflected on the defeat the barbarians inflicted upon imperial Rome: "Whenever the barbarian won, it was because he was already more than half civilized."[9] In the same way that civilization closes itself on the barbarian, when the other is converted by a culture that believes itself to be superior, the condition of the triumphant revolution, the moment when the rebels enter the Winter Palace, is seen when the rebels themselves have been impregnated with all that lines the walls inside.

The Maoists were well aware of this, for was it not the intention of the Chinese Cultural Revolution to force its admirative cadres

---

9.   Fernand Braudel, *The Structures of Everyday Life: The Limits of the Possible* (London: William Collins Sons, 1981), 94.

to break with the political culture they had internalized through their work? Indeed, Lenin also sought to break from the internalized political culture in the post-revolution, carrying this project through as a subterfuge, pretending that violence and humiliation could be instruments for changing cultures and habits.

It is clear that the left is a long way from breaking with patriarchy and colonialism. The search for caudillos and their uncritical devotion to them (Evo Morales, Lula, Rafael Correa, Hugo Chávez), embodies the continuity of a political culture that, a century after the triumph of the Russian Revolution, should have given way to other more horizontal and less hierarchical variables. The Latin American left remains deeply macho, far beyond its own discourses, as evidenced by their refusal to convict such a well-known rapist as Daniel Ortega, the current president of Nicaragua.

Latin America's left movements and governments remain deeply colonial. Take for instance the paternalistic attitude toward Native and Black peoples, people who are considered objects of social "aid" but never subject to an equal footing. In Bolivia, the Movement Toward Socialism (MAS), which is now in power has expressed these sentiments toward the Indigenous organizations Cidob and Conamaq.[10] María Galindo, a Bolivian anarchafeminist, points out the hypocrisy embedded within the much-celebrated plurinationality. Galindo argues that a "Quechua-Aymara hegemony" linked to the MAS is being built in that country, one that is formed on the basis of silencing "the voices of the peoples of the Bolivian East," those who are non-affiliated Indigenous sectors.[11]

10. The Confederation of Indigenous Peoples of eastern Bolivia and the National Council of Ayllus and Markas of Qullasuyu were infiltrated by the police of Evo Morales's government to expel the legitimate leaders and impose those related to the MAS.

11. Radio Deseo, "Análisis Del Discurso Del Presidente Luis Arce En El Aniversario Del Estado Plurinacional," video, January 24, 2022 https://www.youtube.com/watch?v=OaOCeOgV7DI.

The electoral left has also fully embraced the capitalist marketing schemes created to encourage consumerism. An eloquent case is found in the 2016 election campaign in Spain, where Podemos presented a program that, in its format, imitates the catalog of the furniture and home decor company Ikea, with the excuse that it will be the "most read program of democracy."[12] Being inspired by business and marketing strategies is much more than a matter of form as it internalizes advertising values and ends up pairing politics with sales techniques, and the electorate with behaviors similar to those of the consumer.

The sociologist Marcos Roitman believes that the left is always looking for the novel, reinventing itself behind the latest fashion in what he calls a "result-oriented" attitude, determined to seek results that legitimize the left party's agenda even at the risk of emptying it of any substance. That is why he concludes that the left "wants to win power at all costs, but without a project."[13]

The fourth difficulty is that the left avoids conflict, thereby ceasing to fight for transformations, which only occur in the interests of the richest 1 percent, but also leaves the population at the mercy of the system. Social conflict generates awareness, allowing the various sectors to identify the problems that affect them and recognize those who are responsible.

The psychoanalyst and researcher Miguel Benasayag and the philosopher Angélique Del Rey argue that conflict shapes our civilization and that its absence—in societies that aspire for its disappearance—places us in a dire situation of self-destruction: "The denial of conflict can produce barbarism. That is why it

12.   Jorge Otero, "Podemos Imita El Catálogo de Ikea Para Que Su Programa 'Sea El Más Leído de La Democracia,'" *Público*, June 8, 2016, https://www.publico.es/politica/imita-al-catalogo-ikea-programa.html.

13.   Marcos Roitman, "La Nueva, Novísima, Nueva Izquierda Latinoamericana," *La Jornada*, January 17, 2022, https://www.jornada.com.mx/2022/01/17/opinion/016a1pol.

is important to refuse to think separately about conflict and civilization."[14]

In fact, conflict is, on the one hand, the collective power capable of curbing, or limiting, the tendency toward barbarism to which development and progress can lead us. On the other hand, without conflict the novel can never emerge, nor can the collective subjects capable of engendering it emerge. Toward the end of their work, they argue that conflict is the "foundation of life," the force capable of exercising care and at the same time creating new social relations, the new worlds to which those of us who remain anticapitalist aspire to reach. However, the electoral lefts have succumbed to the social and cultural tendency that shuns conflict, seemingly fearing it for a variety of reasons: the risk of losing control of their social bases and what suits the leadership; not wanting to appear as radicals before society, since conflict has been identified with violence; and, finally, because pragmatism leads them to give priority to the institutional scenario, there seems to be no place for conflict because it is considered to be a destabilizing force for institutions. In this way, by nullifying the conflict they slowly decay, diluting themselves within mainstream society, losing the capacity for criticism because they fear isolation and to engage in the proverbial swim against the current that always defined emancipatory movements.

The fifth difficulty is the persistent desire to govern others, something that has become commonplace on the left. This political position contributes to several problems. Governing by definition is a model of oppression, of making decisions that affect other people, replacing them as collective subjects. It also implies leaving aside self-governance or, better, the necessary multiplication of self-governance (in neighborhoods, towns, cities, and in all areas of

---

14. Miguel Benasayag and Angélique Del Rey, *Elogio Del Conflicto* (Buenos Aires: Libros de la Araucaria, 2018), 4.

life) that emancipatory processes entail. Finally, to the extent that it is intended to govern over a social totality, a concept of totality is of a Eurocentric nature, one that fails to contemplate complex realities such as those present in Latin America.[15]

According to Peruvian sociologist Aníbal Quijano, this Eurocentric view assumes that "in a totality the whole has absolute determining primacy over each and every one of the parts" and therefore "there is one and only one logic that governs the behavior of each and every part."[16] However, in Latin America as a whole and in its parts, we find completely different and divergent logics, which makes it impossible for a homogenous transition process to take hold. In my opinion, this fact should lead us to reflect in a totally different way than how European socialism theorized the concept of transition. I will continue to revisit these themes in several parts throughout this book.

The various "parts" in Latin America are each of themselves whole units composed with their own configurations, meaning that they can each have their own relative autonomy, due to both their historical and structural heterogeneity. A whole does exist but is different, not organic as the Eurocentric model perceives it to be, which means that the whole will not be able to move "unilinearly, nor unidirectionally, nor unidimensional, because they are in action, multiple, heterogeneous, and even conflicting impulses or logics of movement."[17] The heterogeneities that Quijano analyzes are found in the spaces of Indigenous and Black peoples, peasants and *mestizos*, in their *quilombos/palenques* communities (the semi-autonomous zones born of historical Black struggles) and in the territories of agrarian families but also in the urban peripheries

---

15. Aníbal Quijano, "The Coloniality of Power and Social Classification," *Journal of World Systems* 6, no. 2 (2000): 342–86.
16. Quijano, "The Coloniality of Power," 296.
17. Quijano, "The Coloniality of Power," 299.

where different peoples have settled as a result of various kinds of migrations. In these spaces, wage relations coexist with those of reciprocity, the various types of easements and the initiatives of small mercantile/families whose work relations have different characteristics than those of wage labor. It is impossible that such diverse and variegated realities can all transition at the same time, moving from one historical scenario and giving way to another in its place. We must consider that there are peoples who are already leaving the capitalist system and are forming worlds very different from the one that still remains hegemonic. Within them, use-values predominate over exchange values, since they do not produce commodities but rather goods that communities require in order to take care of life as a collective. This is the reality of the Zapatista bases of support but also of other pueblos and neighborhood communities that are nevertheless partial and incipient. Identifying these processes has been the object of my work for over three decades, inspired in large part by the Zapatista revolution.

For this reason, the vision of history attributed to Marx (which he himself rejected in his correspondence with Vera Zasulich), consists of the sequence of modes of production (primitive, slave-owning, feudal, capitalist, and communist), corresponds with a historical teleology that assumes that the whole and each of its parts leave entirely from one system in order to enter into another.[18] Impractical as this idea of totality is, so is the concept of hegemony (a subject that Quijano does not address), which presupposes the existence of a homogeneous totality—which the Zapatistas rightly consider a form of oppression—in worlds in which heterogeneity is irreducible to the homogenizing unit. As a result, we can see a new conception of change gaining shape, one where autonomy and

18. Karl Marx and Frederick Engels, *Selected Correspondence* (Moscow: Progress Publishers, 1955). Available at https://www.marxists.org/archive/marx/works/1881/zasulich/draft-1.htm.

self-government displace the old dichotomy between reform and revolution.

I would like to highlight a sixth difficulty, consisting in the loss of historical depth that has polluted the left's political practice, leading to the lack of a long-term vision. I am referring to the immediatism characteristic of those who have surrendered to the dominant culture and way of doing politics in the contemporary moment. The prominent role that we attribute to Indigenous peoples, peasants, and Black peoples is closely linked to their position within an atemporal, circular, and nonlinear space where the idea of progress is alien. Instead, these collective subjects remain committed to living in harmony with the environment, to conserve and not to prey, to care and not to accumulate, refusing to turn nature into a commodity.

Finally, to highlight the relationship between the systemic chaos we are currently experiencing, a period of deep uncertainty that has blinded the future of millions of people, particularly the young, with the resurgence of a certain millenarianism (I cannot find a better word—secular and revolutionary—offering certainties as planks of salvation when everything else around us is sinking). We can see this in a kind of neo-Stalinism among a sector of young university students that has seemingly gained momentum during the pandemic. I know of two cases, that of Ecuador and that of Euskal Herría, but surely they are not the only ones since these trends are global in nature.[19]

These tendencies present two major additional problems: they are unable to accept the failure of socialist revolutions and the role of state centralism in their disastrous drift; and neither can they engage with causes other than the class struggle, such as feminism

---

19.   Euskal Herría refers to a revitalized socialist movement in the Basque region of Spain.

and the modes of resistance presented by Indigenous peoples, some of which are focused on the construction of collective autonomies. A century after Stalinism began to prevail in the international communist movement and half a century after the growth of feminism and Indigenous peoples' rights, history's clock has stopped once again . . . in Moscow in 1930. Thus, a dogmatic Marxism reappears, deeply patriarchal and colonial, entrenched in progress, and in a good part of the doctrines that have already demonstrated their monumental failure.

I firmly believe that the systemic crisis, the growing dictatorial power of the 1 percent and the dogmatic responses to capitalism, can only be overcome through close contact with the most dynamic movements and a predisposition to learn together with the various *abajos* (belows). That is why we seek to follow in the footsteps and inspirations of pueblos on the move (societies in movement), of antipatriarchal and anticapitalist women and youth who, while resisting, create the new worlds that we need to continue existing, to continue living.

✽ ✽ ✽

This book is a compilation of several articles that address the same theme: pueblos organized as collective subjects of resistance to neoliberal capitalism and at the same time creators of new worlds. In the six chapters that follow, the living experience of the peoples themselves serve as the compass for theoretical reflection used to project the type of transition we are currently living, toward the other worlds that are being built and the different ways in which each pueblo defends them.

Societies in Movement Opening Anticolonial Pathways

In this chapter, we are examining the ways in which pueblos in motion have become subjects of decolonization, to the extent that they are disarticulating hierarchical, logocentric, patriarchal, and colonial relations that sustain the regime of capitalist accumulation and domination. Among the various adversaries that they must overcome are state and academic institutions, along with the repressive forces that prop them up. It is only through their critical engagement and confrontation with these institutions that we are able to note the latter's oppressive character, which ends up becoming the first stone on the path of material and epistemic decolonization.

One of the major obstacles to overcome in this anticolonial process is the very concept of *social movement*, and I would go further to include the concept of *antisystemic movement* as well. Both of these concepts were created in a specific context (the United States and Europe) to theorize the collective actions and interactions with the State in those regions. But in no way can they be generalized to understand the movements of people in other parts of the world, particularly those who are grounded in sites that inform their dissidence and resistance; those who sustain their own authorities, build nonstate power, and develop whole networks outside of market social relations to educate, heal, and resolve conflicts.[1]

For a while I used the concept of "societies in movement" to emphasize that what is set in motion in territorialized collective action—miscategorized as social movements—are heterogeneous social relations that contrast the hegemonic ones found in broader society. In other words, societies or "pueblos" in movement captures a dynamic and self-determinate movement that conventional frameworks from Euro-Western thought misses. The use of the concept of "social movement" reifies totality, when in actuality many movements in Latin America set off a motion of their own. These sorts of movements are inherent to the territorially grounded collectives of Indigenous and Black peoples, peasants, and urban popular sectors that inhabit the peripheries of large cities in Latin America. In recent years, witnessing the rise of the Zapatista and Kurdish revolutions, as well as the many processes of self-determination in several Latin American geographies, I have opted for use "pueblos in movement," in the understanding that these are collective subjects that make up different peoples distinguished by their collective differences.[2]

A second obstacle can be found in the spatiotemporal limitation of emancipatory ideas and analyses. To elaborate on this, I introduce the work of the Egyptian sociologist Anouar Abdel-Malek, who is less known in the West for his postcolonial interventions than Edward Said but has presented great insight for understanding the dynamics of the particular and universal. Anouar Abdel-Malek formulates a particular critique of universalism and reminds us that the term "decolonization" is exclusive to the "Western-centrists," because it takes the Western penetration in

---

1. Raúl Zibechi, *Descolonizar: El Pensamiento Crítico y Las Prácticas Emancipatorias* (Montevideo: Alter ediciones, 2020).
2. Raúl Zibechi, *Movimientos Sociales en América Latina: El Mundo Otro en Movimiento* (Málaga: Bajo Tierras Ediciones, 2018).

Asia and Africa as an axis of analysis; that is, "a process of civilization" that is confronted by the resurgence of the East, driven by the processes of national liberation or national revolutions.[3] I engage further with Abdel-Malek's work in the next chapter.

Abdel-Malek was not satisfied with simple denunciation and investigated the ways to overcome colonialism and imperialism. To get out of the universalist abstraction, he focuses on studying the "historical specificity" of oppressed nations, a task that leads him to divide the world between two civilizations or "major circles" (China and Indo-Aryan) and multiple cultural areas or "intermediate circles." Because he considers that "there can be no universal without a comparative framework," he therefore focuses on the dialectic of the specific that allows him to delve into the differences and particularities that all form part of the universal.[4]

Along this path, Abdel-Malek points to the limits of Marxism as a "general sociological conception," since "the application of this method to the advanced industrial societies will not yield up any lasting contribution to the non-Western societies in their hour of renaissance."[5] He writes in the years of Vietnam's victorious resistance to the invasion of the United States and the Chinese Cultural Revolution, which showed divergences from Soviet socialism. However, if Marxism were applied, he argues, "on the basis of historical specificity," it would be an instrument of enormous validity for the understanding of non-Western civilizations. Inspired by his proposal for analyzing historical specificity, I intend to bring forth two concrete developments into the debate that, in my opinion, demonstrate the ongoing process of decolonization. These developments are put forth with the conviction that anticolonial subjects are the

---

3.   Anouar Abdel-Malek, *Social Dialectics*, Vol. 1, *Civilisations and Social Theory* (London: Macmillan Press, 1981), 6.
4.   Abdel-Malek, *Social Dialectics*, 114.
5.   Abdel-Malek, *Social Dialectics*, 117.

only ones capable of decolonizing social relations particularly when they are unraveled within grassroot collectives themselves.

The first development demonstrates the ways in which collective practices (*minga, tequio,* or *guelaguetza*) are situated in places outside of classical political economy, as they seek to displace the individual concept of wage labor and reconstruct another political economy.[6] The second development brings us to the thinking of Kurdish leader Abdullah Öcalan, who is dismantling the center-pieces of Western emancipatory thought—with special emphasis on the struggle of women—from the concrete experience of the peoples of the Middle East.

Decolonizing Critical Thought through Collective Practice

The categories and concepts that fall under political economy in general, and Marxist critique in particular, are based on the individual, on the relationship between the capitalist and the worker as individual subjects. Although both belong to a social class, the relationships they establish are of a personal nature, such as the examples that Marx gives when he analyzes the links between them. The whole structure of the political economy is built on individuals. When Marx defines material production, he says: "The point of departure is not the labour of individuals considered as social labour, but on the contrary the particular kinds of labour of private individuals, i.e., labour which proves that it is universal social labour only by the supersession of its original character in the exchange process."[7]

---

6.   These Indigenous concepts will be further elaborated throughout the text.

7.   Karl Marx, *A Contribution to the Critique of Political Economy*, Marxists Internet Archive, https://www.marxists.org/archive/marx/works/1859/critique-pol-economy.

The working class is therefore a sum of individuals with common interests. The category "wage labor" refers to "a" particular worker who receives a wage for "his" work. In the same way, the commodity "labor power" is individualized to the point that two workers who work in different areas or trades receive different remunerations. Each worker owns his labor power and goes to the market to sell it, as an individual possessor, to an individual buyer.

Private property and the circulation of money are, for Marx and for his followers, a feature of the progress of overcoming primitive society. The use of money, for example, defines a society that is not only developed but also mature, as Marx considers that societies in which there is no money are "historically immature," although they have reached an important degree of development, such as pre-Columbian societies.[8] In "General Introduction to the Critique of Political Economy," Marx states that "bourgeois society is the most complex and developed historical organization of production," adding that, through it, it is possible to develop an "insight into the structure and the relations of production of all formerly existing social formations the ruins and component elements of which were used in the creation of bourgeois society."[9] In short, bourgeois economics provides the key to the old economy, just as "the anatomy of man is a key to the anatomy of the ape." In this sense, progress is moving from lower stages toward higher stages of development.

Marxist analysis, centered on the developed bourgeois society, has shown its validity for the understanding of capitalist social relations at the center of the world system, which effectively "evolved" from the simplest to the most complex forms in societies characterized by high levels of homogeneity. But in no way can the categories

8.   Marx, *A Contribution to the Critique of Political Economy*.
9.   Marx, *A Contribution to the Critique of Political Economy*.

conceptualized for these realities account for what has happened in different worlds, where social relations are founded on other kinds of social realities, that, in Marxist terminology, would be considered remnants of the past. To understand the limits of Marx's analysis of capital, I will use the Zapatista movement as an example, demonstrating how they have developed another kind of political economy as presented by the Insurgent Subcomandante Moisés, in the "Critical Thinking in the Face of the Capitalist Hydra" meeting.[10] In his analysis of "Political Economy from the Zapatista Communities," Subcomandante Moisés traces the path they have traveled from 1983 to the present.[11] In the early years, before the Zapatista Army of National Liberation (EZLN) was formed, the landowners owned the best land with thousands of head of cattle, thanks to the white guards or armed gunmen, with whose help they used to push the peasants into the mountains. To transform their reality, the peasants first recovered the means of production, the land, later deliberating on how they would work it. The peasants ultimately decided on working the land collectively.

All of Moisés's reflections on the economy (in two luminous interventions titled "Political Economy from the Zapatista Communities I and II") revolve around collective practice, on which the whole of life rests for Zapatista communities. But not all productive work is collective: the Zapatista assemblies agree that some days are for the collective and other days "for us," that is, for the family plot.

Among the pueblos, collective work is localized, it is registered in the communities and sometimes among several communities

---

10. Sixth Commission of the EZLN, *Critical Thought in the Face of the Capitalist Hydra I* (Durham, NC: Paper Boat Press, 2016).

11. Subcomandante Insurgente Moisés, "Political Economy from the Zapatista Communities I and II," in *Critical Thought in the Face of the Capitalist Hydra I*.

that collaborate to accomplish a certain task that affects all of them in common. The Zapatistas have multiplied this collective work at all levels of their autonomy:

> The collective work is done at the level of the village, the local level or the community. It is also done at the regional level, as we call it, where the region is a group of 40, 50, or 60 villages. Collective work is also done at the municipal level, by which we mean a group of three, four, or five regions—that is, at the level of the Autonomous Zapatista Municipalities in Rebellion. When we say "the collective work of the zone" we mean the work of all of the municipalities that exist in the five zones, like La Realidad, Morelia, Garrucha, etc.[12]

According to this description, collective practices are carried out throughout the Zapatista territories, a basic feature of their daily lives. It is what has allowed them to build hundreds of schools and health posts, maintain production, cooperatives, and other collective enterprises, as well as build clinics, hospitals, and other health centers. They have also been able to build secondary schools, processing centers for raw material, and the entire material fabric of the hundreds of thousands of Zapatistas who live in more than a thousand communities across forty collective self-governing spaces.

Moisés adds something critical: "collective work doesn't only mean work with Mother Earth." He tells us that collective practice is not only in the means of production, but in all aspects of life, material and nonmaterial. The construction of self-governance is based on collective work: from health and education to justice, power, and good governance boards (*juntas de buen gobierno*). How

---

12. Moisés, "Political Economy from the Zapatista Communities I," in *Critical Thought*, 65–66.

does this take place? The people in charge of health, *hueseras* (bone healers), midwives, and curandera/os (healers who work with medicinal plants), whom they refer to as "promoters," are elected in the assembly of the community, not because of their abilities but because it is their time to provide service, to support their community in these responsibilities. They do not receive remuneration but through collective work the community assures their subsistence, cultivates their *milpa* (crop growing plot), and supports them with food and covers their needs. The same happens with the promoters of education and all the tasks necessary for the reproduction of life. That is why Moisés says that "the pay" is the community care of the *milpa*, the *frijolar* (bean field), the coffee plantation, or the pasture. The assembly also makes use of collective work to make decisions and sustain those it elects. In other words, the community supports its representatives through collective work.

One of the great contributions of Zapatismo is the way they have extended collective work to all the ways they exercise autonomy: local or community, municipal, regional, and the bigger zones. The Zapatistas who make up municipalities and good government juntas also operate collectively, relying on this model to meet, make decisions, and sustain themselves materially. This is not a staggered system where one level of autonomy sustains the level above, but rather each are set up as interdependent collectives. In short, collective labor replaces money, the very foundation of capitalism, and there is no political economy that properly reflects this economy.

"If there is no organization there is nothing."[13] Collective work is not decided by a central command or a centralized institution, which would be tantamount to reproducing a state system. It is the

---

13.   Subcomandante Insurgente Moisés, "Resistance and Rebellion III," in *Critical Thought*, 152.

villages, the regions, the autonomous municipalities, and the zones that must come together to decide how the work should be implemented and how it should be carried out. For example, there are families that have few children and others that have many, and so it is up to them to discuss how much time each family can spend working for themselves and how much for the collective and so on to address all the problems that arise.

As Gladys Tzul Tzul points out, regarding the Indigenous peoples in Guatemala, communal service is not paid because "it is the obligatory work that we all have to do for the sustenance of life in common."[14] This obligation also applies to the Indigenous communal government assemblies as well, "where the *K'ax K'ol* (a k'iche' concept for a kind of collective practice) is the foundation on which the assembly rests and where the systems of communal government are produced. This is where the full participation of all takes place."[15]

At this point, it should be noted that the communal assembly is very different from the assembly of urban workers or that of the neighborhood assemblies. It is mandatory, because it is an additional form of collective work. The communal authorities are decision bearers of the assemblies, to the point that "there is no dissociation between communal authority and communal assembly."[16]

The Zapatista system is decentralized. In each region, the town/community collectively decides how to spend the money from the harvest sale; they decide on whether to save it in the communal bank or spend it on some need for their movement. Communal life and values, on which Zapatismo is based, rely upon

---

14. Gladys Tzul Tzul, "Sistemas de Gobierno Comunal Indígena: La Organización de La Reproducción de La Vida," *El Apantle* 1 (October 2015): 132.

15. Tzul, "Sistemas de Gobierno Comunal Indígena," 133.

16. Gladys Tzul Tzul, "La Producción de La Autoridad Comunal Indígena. Breve Esbozo Para Guatemala," *El Apantle* 2 (October 2016): 29.

a broad decentralization that allows for the expression of the specificities of each geography and every pueblo.[17]

> For the collective work projects that we are discussing, what has really helped us is working in the following manner: dividing the month into 10 days of collective work and 20 days of family work. Each person agrees. Some places might decide differently, 5 days for collective work and 25 for the work of the family. But each place makes their agreement at the level of the community or the region or autonomous municipality or the zone. These are the four levels at which the collective work projects take place, which is to say there are four levels of assemblies, which is to say four levels at which to come to agreement.[18]

A decentralized economy, controlled by assemblies and collective labor, reproduces another society, one in which concepts such as property, wage and abstract labor, surplus value and accumulation do not exist. Developing an analysis of a political economy centered on collective work is the challenge for contemporary critical thought. This challenge involves the decolonization of categories based on the exploited individual, the wage worker, replacing it instead with a kind of work that has no reference in previous currents of critical thought. This challenge concerns not only economics, but all disciplines, since all take the individual or the citizen as a starting point.

The Zapatista support bases do not have private ownership of the land, nor of any of the means of production. They only

---

17. At least five native peoples converge within the EZLN, in addition to mestizos, who live in mountain, jungle, and intermediate regions.
18. Moisés, "Political Economy from the Zapatista Communities II," in *Critical Thought*, 86.

administer the lands recovered through collective struggle, as well as manage all material creations (schools, clinics, cooperatives, etc.) through collective work. This work does not produce any exchange values (they only sell a part of the production on the market), as any of the money collected is reabsorbed as use-value. For this reason, they keep monetary exchange to a minimum, as use-value exchanges are the norm. Therefore, there is no abstract work, only concrete work; nor is there the exploitation or extraction of surplus value. Among the Zapatistas there is no capital, as collective labor does not value capital, making accumulation and capital obsolete.

So, these new worlds—of which Zapatismo is only a part of, albeit one of the most developed and extensive—deserve a new kind of political economy, one that no longer depends on what happened in the past socialist countries. The reflections produced by "real socialism" were symmetrical to those of the political economy of bourgeois society: it conceptualized, for example, a socialist mode of production, the "law of primitive socialist accumulation," and so on. All of its categories were a reflection of bourgeois economy in a socialist variant, to the point that "it would seem that in respect of the distribution and investment of new productive resources . . . [socialism is] following in the footsteps of capitalism."[19]

It has been through the organization of the bases of support, the recovery of the means of production through collective struggle, and the extension of collective work into all spheres and tasks of life that allow communities to overcome or decolonize the analytical categories elaborated by Marx in his "Critique of Political Economy."

---

19.   Eugene Preobrazhensky, *The New Economics* (Oxford: Oxford University Press, 1966), 199.

Decolonizing Feminism from Kurdistan

Since at least 2012, the Kurdish Freedom movement has capti-
vated and reinvigorated critical thought and praxis around the
world. Known as the Rojava Revolution, or more recently, the
Revolution of the Autonomous Administration of North and East
Syria (AANES), this revolution in historical Kurdistan is recovering ancestral knowledge to drive their contemporary struggles. The
Kurdish worldview, including many of their practices and priorities, has been undergoing a transformation during the Kurds long
struggle for liberation. I would like to dwell on two aspects that I
consider important anticolonial contributions to critical thought:
their formulation of a "women's science" or *jineology*, which shows
the outstanding role women have had in the Kurdish movement
as a whole; and the works of Abdullah Öcalan, a key thinker of the
Kurdish Worker's Party, the precursor to the AANES.

AANES's evolution traces the contours of Abdullah Öcalan's
theoretical work, which he has developed to criticize and detach
himself from the theoretical-political heritage of Marxism-Leninism
in an effort to open up new currents of critical thought. Resistance
against colonialism/imperialism, patriarchy, and capitalism made
the Kurdish movement realize that it needed to change and overcome ideas the PKK (Kurdish Workers Party) had embraced since
its founding in the 1970s. I want to emphasize that this has not only
been the result of theoretical developments, and the emancipation
of Kurdish women is not due to Öcalan (as a typical and presumed
infallible caudillo [strongman]), as some have maliciously sug-
gested from the West, but rather it has been the result of the direct
participation of a people struggling for their survival.

Kurdish women established this new position in society first
through their participation in the collective resistance, where they
took off into the mountains to fight, an experience that "took them

away from the conventional conservative roles and values, where they experienced new ways of understanding life at the individual and collective level."[20] In 1987, the first Kurdish women's organization, the Union of Patriotic Women of Kurdistan (YJWK), was founded in Hanover, Germany. While they embraced Western feminism, they were not limited by it, as they grounded themselves in Kurdish and Middle Eastern traditions. But arguably, the decisive moment of the Kurdish movement and the PKK coming together with feminism was the creation of the Kurdish women's army in 1993, because "it generated a space in which women who wanted to get out of the spiral of capitalist modernity and patriarchy could rely on themselves."[21]

Kurdish women emphasized that participation in this army "created very strong experiences," to the extent that they had a double struggle, one that they turned inward and one outward: While Kurdish women fought for their existence against the nation-state, they also fought men for their own place on the frontline with the guerrillas. The ideological struggles among the guerrillas demonstrated the way that the interlocking systems of patriarchy, capitalism, and the State had seeped through all of society. Therefore, it was not enough to understand the system by simply looking through the lens of class struggles and national liberation movements.[22]

Without experiencing the internal contradictions and the patriarchy that pervaded the unified revolutionary organizations,

---

20. Movimiento de mujeres del Kurdistón, "El Movimiento Kurdo de Mujeres," in *La Revolución Ignorada: Liberación De La Mujer, Democracia Directa Y Pluralismo Radical En Oriente Medio*, ed. Descontrol (Barcelona: Descontrol, 2015), 51.

21. Comité de Jineolojî Europa, "Jineolojî" (n.p.: Comité de Mujeres En Solidaridad Con Kurdistán, 2017), 26, https://pueblosencamino.org/wp-content/uploads/2018/02/Librito-Jineologi-.pdf.

22. Comité de Jineolojî Europa, "Jineolojî," 27.

they would not have been able to take the steps that led them to form a complete network of autonomous organizational structures, both in their militia and in broader society, through the power they established in 2012 in Rojava, northern Syria.[23] On March 8, 1995, during the first Kurdish women's congress, the Women's Liberation Union (YAJK) was created, and has since played a leading role in the organization and politicization of women in the region. Four years later, the Kurdistan Working Women's Party (PJKK) was created, the first party of women and the result of their ever-growing self-organization.

The Kurdish women's movement has been strengthening its roots in many sectors and communities of the region. In 2005, the High Council of Women (KJB) was formed. It later became the Kurdistan Women's Communities (KJK, where the first K stands for *kom*, or community in Kurdish traditions). Not to be confused with a Western-style feminist organization, the KJK is set up as "a system that brings together the perspectives and responses of women's struggles in the four parts of Kurdistan" as it seeks to break from the patriarchal system in order for Kurdish women to empower themselves "to obtain an autonomous identity across all social conditions."[24]

Although jineology is inspired by feminism, it overcomes it by rooting itself in local cultures, not in an attempt to mechanically reproduce them, but to enrich an emancipatory work with an anti-systemic perspective, coming together with similar processes of liberation, including the anticolonial and antipatriarchal struggles.

"When feminists examine the East from the West, they often fall into blind spots by not incorporating the theories that emerged

---

23.   Rojava is most recently referred to as the Autonomous Administration of North and East Syria (AANES) to reflect its inclusivity.

24.   Comité de Jineolojî Europa, "Jineolojî," 32.

from Eastern literatures."[25] It is clear that the experience of Kurdish women in the European diaspora had two seemingly contradictory consequences: it connected them with feminism though led them to reject its Eurocentric ideas in order to deepen their ties to women in their pueblos.

Kurdish women in the PKK took up both of these aspects. They reject the temptation of Western feminism to separate itself from society, which led most feminist currents to be integrated into the capitalist system up to the point that it accepted some of the demands of these feminist movements. The capitalist system co-opted the feminist movements, ultimately creating islands of "freedom," including sexual freedom. Sexuality was initially analyzed in feminist discourses as a problem of slavery and domination of society, but later came to be discussed as a question of liberal freedom. "Sexual freedom" has been handled as an individualistic issue, and because of this it has not been possible to develop a culture of open sexuality that is truly free of domination and slavery.[26]

Kurdish women's critical feminism, inspired by jineology, seeks to transform the whole of society, including men. It asserts that Western feminism is reproducing sexual politics rather than transforming them and that the formation of separate spaces for women leaves aside the transformation of men. It concludes that feminism "has been created as a movement that mainly resists and rejects."[27] In short, we are told that there can be no emancipation of women if there is no emancipation of society, leading Kurdish women to take up an anti-system position that is at the same time "anti-militarist, anti-power, anti-sexist, anti-racist, and anti-fascist."[28]

---

25.   Comité de Jineolojî Europa, "Jineolojî," 32.
26.   Comité de Jineolojî Europa, "Jineolojî," 39.
27.   Comité de Jineolojî Europa, "Jineolojî," 40.
28.   Comité de Jineolojî Europa, "Jineolojî," 37.

The work of politicization, along with the diffusion of jineology throughout Kurdish society, has led to the development of coleadership, or the sharing of power between men and women across various political organizations. This has resulted in egalitarian representation, which has permeated all sectors of society. Once again, it is the guerrilla experiences at the root of the changes.

"The autonomous organization of the women guerrillas in the mountains of Kurdistan have created a communal model of life for women, not only in the mountains but also in broader society."[29] In that sense, they point out, it is not the same to separate from society in order to feel free, as it is to live freed in a transformed society.

Rojava has seen remarkable progress following the formation of the Women's Defense Units (YPJ) in 2012. For many young women, participation in the armed brigades was a way to escape oppressive traditional environments and live in spaces of personal and collective freedom. Undoubtedly, their successful participation in the fight against Daesh (ISIL) earned them the respect of their communities. However, "they believe that the day will come when an organization like the YPJ will no longer be necessary, since they will be able to be integrated into the (co-ed) People's Defense Units (YPG) without having to denounce their restrictions."[30]

Gender parity in all structures and organizations (a process that the EZLN also takes up) has led to the organized duality in the Popular Council System. Women's Councils have been set up to build out a network of communes coordinated through their own councils, aspiring to have all those living in territories, neighborhoods, and villages participating in decision making. These councils have the ability to resolve conflicts involving women (such as domestic violence) according to their own criteria and can veto

---

29. Comité de Jineolojî Europa, "Jineolojî," 38.
30. Editorial Descontrol, "Las Transformaciones Sociales," in *La Revolución Ignorada*, 153.

decisions of the broader People's Councils. The kind of power they are building through this structure is of vital importance, as conflicts involving women are of imminent concern for movements all throughout the globe.

The Kurdish women's movement, embodied in jineology, provided the material basis for Öcalan's theoretical work captured in the remarkable text, "Killing the Male." Although the original book has not yet been translated, a synthesis of the text can be accessed in jineology's work: "Killing the male is practically the basic principle of socialism. In this way, power, partial government, inequality, and intolerance are killed," writes Öcalan.[31] He adds: "The militancy of the PKK is linked to the idea of killing the male." The proposal to "kill the male" concerns the whole of society being involved in the liberation of women. The collective subject of that "killing" is all people, to the extent that what is ultimately sought is "the emancipation of women and society as a whole."[32]

No revolutionary movement in the world has reached such a degree of development with regard to women's liberation as the Kurdish movement. It is a movement that understands the enormous liberating power contained in the struggle of women and they formulate it in such as simple way: "the field of gender relations is the place from which liberation and revolutionary developments will be carried out."[33] They are talking about profound changes in the relationships between men and women, which was always the goal of feminism.

Abdullah Öcalan's role is fundamental in this process as he is producing a complete reworking of critical thought inherited from Marx. In his vast reconstruction of history, Öcalan presents a worldview centered upon the Middle East, the place from which

---

31. Comité de Jineolojî Europa, "Jineolojî," 65.
32. Comité de Jineolojî Europa, "Jineolojî," 43.
33. Comité de Jineolojî Europa, "Jineolojî," 66.

the Kurdish people are leading their revolution. This aspect is central. Aimé Césaire argued half a century ago that a history that starts from the peoples who inhabited Mesopotamia can only enrich the history of all peoples, as particularities add to the universal. Césaire refused both to be lost by "walled segregation in the particular" and to collapse into "the universal." His choice was for "a universal enriched by all that is particular, a universal enriched by every particular," as he ends his letter to Maurice Thorez in 1956.[34]

Öcalan's thought is tributary to the women's movement and also to the fall of Soviet socialism and the decolonization drive of the Kurdish movement. Among his most notable contributions is his critique of economism present in Marxism and in all general tendencies of critical thought. Contrary to those who believe that the birth of capitalism is the "natural" result of economic development, Öcalan considers it the result of the growth of military and political power, which he considers a "modern link of the tradition whereby a band of looters gathered by and around the strong man seizes the social values generated by mother-woman."[35] In Öcalan's vision of history, which is inspired by the historian Fernand Braudel, violence was and is the driving force of capital accumulation. He goes on to argue that in the places where the colonial wars took place, there were no economic rules behind primitive accumulation: "Political economy is the most fraudulent and predatory monument of fictive intelligence, developed to disguise the speculative character of capitalism."[36] Öcalan concludes that "capitalism is not economy, but power," which is based on the concentration of force, armed and unarmed, capable of confiscating the surpluses produced by society.

---

34. Aimé Césaire, "Letter to Maurice Thorez," *Social Text* 28, no. 2 (2010): 152.
35. Abdullah Öcalan, *Manifesto for a Democratic Civilization*, Vol. II, *Capitalism: The Age of Unmasked Gods and Naked Kings* (Porsgrunn, Norway: New Compass Press, 2017), 66.
36. Öcalan, *Manifesto*, Vol. II, 67.

It seems like the emphasis that Öcalan places on the centrality of politico-military power in capitalism's early formation is drawn from his study of the Kurdish women's movement. Something similar can be said about his analysis of the nation-state, which he considers to be a particular kind of power that originates in capitalist civilization. In tune with women's movements across the world that have all changed societies without access to state power, Öcalan develops a deep antistatist position that leads him to reject, among other things, the concept of hegemony as an analytical instrument and definitive praxis from which change happens in the world. "Domination is power and power cannot be achieved without establishing its control, which in turn cannot be achieved without force."[37] This positionality stems from the connection Öcalan makes between the role of the woman-mother—which he thinks of alongside land—and the centrality of use-value [as opposed to market value] he finds in these movements, whose economies, "unlike the contemporary capitalist system, serve to cover the basic needs of society." "In contrast to the order of capital, the economy was the area where society's material needs are attained. The reason for its remaining within the domain of use-value for such a long time is the communal order. Social cohesion can only be governed on the principle that everyone's life should be guaranteed."[38] This structure contrasts the system of profit-driven production and the accumulation of power with the "gift economy," or the *don* (giving), as we call it in Latin America.

Öcalan argues that profit-driven economies led to the destruction of the "pre-civilized society," which in his opinion was synonymous with the woman-mother. These societies were replaced when the male figure converted into the hunter, and

---

37. Öcalan, *Manifesto*, Vol. II, 241.
38. Öcalan, *Manifesto*, Vol. II, 288.

"conflict with the male slowly began to develop," a disruption that flowed through the state when agricultural surpluses allowed for it.[39] The previous society, anchored in the centrality of the woman-mother, was destroyed by "the beginning of commercialization and commerce, which penetrated through the veins of the colonies, leading to an accelerated dissolution of societies, as commodities, exchange value, and property become widespread."

Öcalan's understanding of the centrality of use-value and community in history places his work in dialogue with other pueblos in movement, particularly that of the Zapatista territories of Chiapas and Nasa of the Cauca region in Colombia. The gift economy of the Kurdish, which Öcalan mentions, is comparable to the centrality of the barter system in the *minga hacia adentro* system, which the Regional Indigenous Council of Cauca (CRIC) relied on during the pandemic.[40]

The CRIC in Colombia brings together about two hundred thousand people from eight ethnic groups (Nasa, Totoró, Guambiano, Yanacona, Coconuco, Epigara, Inga, and Pupenense) that occupy just over five hundred thousand hectares in eighty-four *resguardos* (territories), which are governed by 115 *cabildos* (collective authorities). They have also equipped eleven associations of councils that coordinate and administer the numerous territorial areas. In 1971, after the massive recovery of lands in Colombia, CRIC was created to incorporate them as collective property, expand the protected homelands, and strengthen lobbying in support of these territorial formations. Among its programmatic objectives are the training of its own teachers, the creation of economic and community enterprises, and a health and justice system anchored in Indigenous traditions and culture.

---

39. Öcalan, *Manifesto*, Vol. II, 133.
40. *Minga hacia adentro* or inward minga refers to closing off a local territory and relying on self-sustaining communal practices.

The community economy is organized around community enterprises and shops, associations, agricultural colleges, and various projects of the collectives and groups of families that work in very diverse activities: from dairy, livestock, and fish farming agroindustries to small-scale mining, management of water sources and forests, and ecotourism. All of them are owned by the communities and are managed collectively.

It should be noted that there is no state ownership or large enterprises with a high concentration of fixed capital and workers, but a combination of family, affiliated, and community units in the area. In the municipality of Toribío, with just over thirty thousand inhabitants, they have managed to launch seventy fish units: 51 percent of which are family units, 40 percent are associative, and 9 percent community.[41]

Despite limited resources, trout production has reached massive levels, allowing the community to not only supply the families of the municipality but also to "export" to external supermarkets, two from the region and even abroad. In the municipality of Toribío there are three Indigenous reservations (Tacueyó, Toribío, and San Francisco), each of them being directed by a cabildo elected by the *comuneros*.

The trout is processed by the Juan Tama community enterprise, created in 1997 "by the young community of the reservation," promoted by the municipality run by Indigenous Nasa, and financed by the three councils, the "Nasa Project," and international cooperation.[42] It seems necessary to emphasize at this point that despite

41. Kwe'sx Toritrucha, "Pisicultores Del Territorio Ancestral de Toribío: Kwe'sx Toritrucha—Armonia y Equilibrio Con La Madre Tierra," Kwe'sx Toritrucha (blog), August 28, 2017, https://kewextoritrucha .wordpress.com/2017/08/28/pisicultores-del-territorio-ancestral-de -toribio-kwesx-toritrucha.
42. In 1980, the Nasa Project emerged in Toribío "to respond to the division that existed between the reservations of Toribío, Tacueyó, and San

being a "large" company (due to the size of production in a small municipality), they have managed to ensure that management does not leave the hands of the communities. Something similar happens with other ventures, which are guided by the principles of respect for nature and the Nasa worldview.

The surpluses are usually used to fill the needs of the reservation, defined by the authorities of the cabildo in agreement with the communities. The Cabildo de Toribío, for example, defined through the Nasa Project that the community economy should benefit families, support groups that do not have land, generate employment, and "build a common fund to support other projects that arise in the organizational process of the community."[43] In this way, they have been able to set up community shops, small businesses that sell or produce a variety of things such as dairy products, fruit juices and vegetable stands from community farms, and have recently purchased their first mode of transportation.

These personal economies are a way reintroducing the woman-mother—returning here to the concept of Öcalan—although this role takes up a meaning beyond the sex of a person as it can be taken up by anyone. For Öcalan, capitalism is not the consequence of any natural "development" of the economy

---

Francisco, encouraged by political issues and partisan interests that prevented the advance of the organization and the recognition of Indigenous people." See Asociación de Cabildos Indígenas del Norte del Cauca (ACIN), "Proyecto Nasa: Resguardos de Toribío, San Fransisco y Tacueyó—Tortuga," Grupo Tortuga (blog), January 12, 2007, https://www.grupotortuga.com/Proyecto-Nasa-Resguardos-de. The Nasa Project aims to work in three directions: awareness through education and training, community participation through community organization, and integral development with programs and projects that cover the totality of human beings and Mother Earth. It was the first of several life plans or long-term programs that address health, education, etc. that some councils are endowed with organizing.

43. ACIN, "Proyecto Nasa."

driven by technological evolution, as Marx argued in *The Poverty of Philosophy*: "The hand-mill gives you society with the feudal lord; the steam-mill, society with the industrial capitalist." Instead Öcalan argues that capitalism is the result of politico-military and cultural tradition to "usurp social values."[44] His argument places the "forty thieves" (a reference to the forty delegates at the Cairo conference in 1921 that carved up the Middle East after the fall of the Ottoman Empires) at the center of capitalism's rise, instead of technologies. In this way, everything changes; history and its current reality take on other forms, emerging from the opacity in which the political economy had obscured. For Öcalan, these thieves do not simply steal to enrich themselves, they usurp what he calls "social values," most significantly the place of women in society.

Lords and masters come from this group of thieves, Öcalan argues, along with a modern bourgeoisie enriched by the colonial wars of conquest that manufactures a political economy disguised as a science that seeks to hide the essence of capitalism. Therefore, the birth of capitalism does not come about through natural economic forces but rather through authoritarian figures who seek to impose a logic of concentrated power from the outside.

It is here that I see a point of convergence between the emancipatory practice of the support bases of the Zapatista, the original peoples organized in the CRIC, and the theoretical and concrete Kurdish experience. This praxis should not be misinterpreted as a kind of return to primitivism driven by some kind of nostalgia or romanticism. Centering use-value and the perspectives of women comes from the desire and need to overcome capitalism, to resist it; it should be understood as a struggle against the dispossession and inhumanity of capitalism.

---

44. ACIN, "Proyecto Nasa."

Pueblos/societies in movement are not looking to find a lost idyllic society; it is not a type of nostalgia for a world that already was or one they wish for, but something more transcendent. In order to overcome the current state, it is imperative to recover the type of world that has been marginalized for exploitation. Their imperative is the recovery of a society based on the use values of each community. In this effort to sustain life, they find alternative realities that refer to another logic, another ethic, and another way of life.

Toward a "Civilization of Freedom"?

Renowned French historian and social theorist Fernand Braudel was quite skeptical about rapid and irreversible changes: "I do not on the whole believe that social change happens quickly, in sudden bursts. Even revolutions are not complete breaks with the past."[45] Changes at the top, such as the advent of new layers of managers, he argues, often reinforce the established order. It establishes a dialectic between short and long term, between disruptive events and continuities, as cultures slowly mutate. In the study of social movement, it would be like the dialogue that happens between uprisings and insurrections and the construction of a new political culture, processes that converge or decouple according to a priori and unpredictable happenings.

Braudel often uses the concepts of civilization and culture, which he considers "interchangeable in most contexts."[46] This thought distances itself from vulgar Marxism that places culture in the superstructure, subordinate to the relations of production, a process Braudel argues, is always acute: "Culture is the oldest

---

45. Fernand Braudel, *Perspective of the World* (London: William Collins Sons & Co, 1984), 61.
46. Braudel, *Perspective of the World*, 65.

character in human history: economies succeed each other, political institutions crumble, societies replace each other, but civilization continues along its way." He ends with a kind of wise man's assertion: "Civilization is the grandfather, the patriarch of world history."[47]

If there is something on earth capable of limiting the expansionist voracity of capitalism and any other economy, Braudel argues, it is culture that is capable of achieving what society and politics are unable to do. Braudel contends that cultures simultaneously bring together three variables in both a loose and concrete juncture.

The pueblos/societies in movement mentioned above emerged out of a decades-old struggle and their cultural practices are giving rise to new kinds of politics that are creating buffers against the historical efforts to contain and crush them. After a long and intense century of struggle, feminist cultural principles have made their way into broader society, producing long-lasting changes and subversions to patriarchy. Meanwhile, Indigenous peoples and movements are presenting new decolonizing subjects in Latin America [and in a resurgent Turtle Island] reproducing integral social relations (which professional theorists have described as *buen vivir* in Latin America), as an alternative to the civilizational crisis of capitalism.

Zapatismo is a kind of Indigeneity, one of the most well-known in a vast constellation of autonomous and self-governing creations found in thousands of communities. Zapatismo did not invent collectivity, but it had the virtue of understanding its emancipatory potential and sought to multiply it across some of the most diverse spaces, to the point that they have shaped their world and configured an unmistakable culture and way of doing politics, from the smallest of practices to the most extensive and complex. When their bases of support, including schoolchildren, are asked a question,

---

47. Braudel, *Perspective of the World*, 65.

they first consult each other, and only after they have collectively found an answer does someone respond.

The PKK did not invent feminism. Kurdish women who were exiled to the mountains learned it out of necessity, not ideology. They adapted it to their particular Middle Eastern historical traditions and cultures, and subsequently multiplied it until they brought jineology into each and every one of the cantons and neighborhoods in their revolution. They have deepened their understanding of women's oppression to such an extent that they claim that the State was created on the domestication of women, and "killing the male" is the fundamental core of the revolutionary movement.

It is possible that we are at the dawn of something new, something so novel that we do not yet have a name for it. If the concept of "social movements" seems inadequate, then that of "pueblos/societies in movement" may also be insufficient, since they are not simply moving to mobilize and to change the inherited material and symbolic place. The power of both collective subjects—rebellious women and peoples in movement—has allowed them to become the main force of this new dawn. In many ways, they have become the greatest fear of the elites, since they have illuminated a road toward the decolonization/depatriarchalization of social relations, processes so closely intertwined that they do not find it possible to dismantle one without intervening in the other.[48]

As Western civilization falters, a new "civilization of freedom" (what Öcalan calls "democratic civilization") rooted in the common history of humankind may be resurfacing. Torn apart by colonialism and capitalism (with the functional support of patriarchy), this new civilization resurfaces with all the restorative power of communal life. Öcalan's theorization that we should "conceptualize the

---

48. María Galindo, *Feminismo Urgente: ¡A Despatriarcar!* (Buenos Aires: Lavaca, 2013).

social forms prior to the formation of state and civilization, as well as the structures that later existed outside the state," breaks from the common implication of society and the State as complimentary elements, such as is the case in sociology and Marxism.[49] Öcalan instead finds these elements contradictory.

At this point it is necessary to reconceptualize what we understand by colonialism through the historical and contemporary reality of Latin America. Bolivian philosopher Luis Tapia argues that colonialism "is the superposition of societies under relations of domination and exploitation."[50] Based on the historical experience of Upper Peru (present-day Bolivia) and the whole of the Andean region, Tapia establishes three characteristics of colonialism on which he argues that not only has colonialism not ended but that it has intensified, establishing himself as a theorist far from post-colonial and even more so from those who take up the conceptual framing of coloniality.

Luis Tapia's analysis of internal colonialism focused on Bolivia but presents a lens from which to view the Latin American reality. His analysis, whereby states colonize regions or populations within their own borders, goes beyond much of the contemporary critiques of Latin America's metapolitics. In recognizing an entrenched internal colonialism Tapia is in effect pulling back the veil of progressive policies, seeing through the deceptive rhetoric of Latin American leadership and their sympatric academic comrades.

The first characteristic of internal colonialism that Tapia puts forth, which he considers the most important feature of perpetual colonialism, comes from the transformation of agrarian communities into semi-extractivist peoples.[51] In the process of extractivism,

---

49. Öcalan, *Manifesto for a Democratic Civilization*, Vol. II, 284.
50. Luis Tapia, *Dialectica del Colonialism Interno* (Madrid: Traficantes de Sueños, 2022), 225.
51. Tapia, *Dialectica del Colonialism Interno*, 225.

a dominated society (former agrarian communities) work under a new kind of subjugation, thus continuing a relationship that has gone uninterrupted for five centuries.

The second consists of the disruption to self-governance, which was one of the main organizational structures of original peoples prior to conquest. While colonialism did not produce a complete destruction of original forms of self-governance, it succeeded in bringing together some structures of communal authority of the conquered societies in order to ensure a tribute-paying society. Although community production and organization were preserved at the micro level, including the *ayllu*, community, or *marka* scale, in the higher or macro scale, their collective unity was broken up as a part of the conquest: The destruction of communal organizing at the macro level led to a strengthening of productive and social structures at the micro and regional level.[52] However, the macro-level break up led to a partial change of their cultures, a consequence of the loss of a macro-articulation of their political dimensions of self-governance as a result of the imperial power imposed on them.[53]

Despite the change at the higher level, micro-level self-governance and communality has been a key organizing structure in some of the most notable political movements of the last two centuries, since the rebellions of Túpac Katari and Túpac Amaru and, most recently, the diffusion of the Tiwanaku Manifesto in 1973, which gave rise to the contemporary Katarist current in Bolivia.[54]

---

52. The Ayllu and Marka are social organizing forms commonly found in the Andes, from Quechua and Aymara peoples, respectively.

53. Tapia, *Dialectica del Colonialism Interno*, 229.

54. "Katarist" refers to members of Katari Party, a political movement formed in the 1970s in Bolivia. Named after the ancestral site of Tiwanaku, the "Tiwanaku Manifesto" was a statement put out by the Katarista movement that recovered ancestral memory in its critique

The third characteristic that Tapia points to is the establishment of a hierarchy of societies, given that "the colonial relationship is a relationship between societies." This colonial relationship involves a refusal to recognize the conquered peoples as a society as well as denying their humanity through the institution of racism. As part of this colonial domination, the authoritative or governing structures of conquered societies are hierarchical in nature, which can be observed in the way authorities seek the recognition of those above them in order to maintain their privileges, either material or symbolic, over their subordinates. In the colonial period, local *caciques* or Indigenous authorities acted as mediators between the two (Republic of Indians/Republic of Spaniards), preserving the colonial order.

That is why liberation or decolonization for original peoples goes through a dual process of recovering the past and a recognition of the ways in which domination by local authorities has been internalized from the colonial past. In this way, I find a comparable emancipatory processes between feminist women and Indigenous peoples: both patriarchal and colonial domination have been so deeply internalized to the point that they are naturalized. This is why the emancipatory processes of both these movements seek to understand domination in order to dismantle and disarm it, to "disarticulate each and every one of the layers of oppression that hold us back."[55]

In line with many principal thinkers and leaders of Indigenous movements across the continent, Tapia points out that overcoming the colonial relationship requires the rearticulation or recovery of the political dimension that was suppressed by the conqueror. This rearticulation would necessitate an update to the various modes of

---

of neoliberalism and the State. The current governing body of Bolivia traces its lineage to this movement.

55. Tapia, *Dialectica del Colonialism Interno*, 229.

autonomy and self-governance that were lost. Zapatismo is doing just that through the juntas de buen gobierno, as are the Kurds in their autonomous communities found in the cantons Afrin, Jazira, and Kobane, now codified in a constitutional charter.[56] In addition to these better-known movements, this path has also been taken up by diverse peoples and communities throughout the Latin American region, from the inhabitants of Cherán (Mexico) to the Wampis of the northern Peruvian Amazon, as well as other lowland and mountain peoples, non-Indigenous peasant communities, and urban migrants.

However, decolonization cannot simply reconstitute the old forms of self-government with their respective authorities. The State has deeply entrenched modes of extractivism and capitalism within peoples' territories, which is why a complete transformation of the way governance is carried out has become imperative. It has been women's antipatriarchal struggles that have called attention to how attempts to decolonize without this consideration would be an anachronism that would lead to the construction of new modes of oppression. In the past, struggles for the reconstitution of the lifeways of historically subjugated peoples were truncated by repression and genocide. More recently, subtle modes of cooptation have been established: for example, with ideas like "plurinational states" meaning the capture and codification of plurinationality by the State, serving only to maintain and reinforce the main features of the hegemonic colonial culture.[57]

❀ ❀ ❀

---

56. Kurdish Institute, "Charter of the Social Contract in Rojava (Syria)," Kurdish Institute website, February 7, 2014, https://www.kurdishinstitute.be/en/charter-of-the-social-contract.

57. Luis Tapia, "Una Reflexión Sobre la Idea de Estado Plurinacional," *Osal* 7, no. 22 (September 2007).

One of the most hopeful and inspiring features of the movements of our time is the fact that these societies-in-movement and women-in-rebellion are not repeating the precepts of previous struggles that were concerned with seizure of state power in order to carry out structural transformations. The two cases analyzed above, as well as many others that I have documented over the last two decades, show different paths to those previously known.[58] What is being born within these societies-in-movement is quite different from what the socialist revolutions of the twentieth century produced. "One of the main reasons that subservience goes unchallenged," reflects Luis Tapia, "is the normalization of routine, that is, the result of being born and living in a context that has been organized by structures of inequality and discrimination governed by social and political hierarchies."[59]

What kind of society is currently being formed in territories where more or less egalitarian relations between men and women predominate, or amalgamate around collective work? What will people be like after prolonged periods of self-governance and self-management, not only at the local/community level, but in large regions and territories? Critical thought is far off from discerning the political culture of individuals and collectives that have been growing for over three decades; in spaces where people are consciously working against inequality and condemning all kinds of discrimination, that is, where colonial and patriarchal relations are questioned.

What kind of politics and economies are born from the collective work carried out in Zapatista territory? How will we name them? What different politics and forms of power are born of the guerrilla brigades composed of only women in Rojava? Can we

---

58. Raúl Zibechi, *Movimientos sociales en América Latina: El mundo otro en movimiento* (Málaga: Bajo Tierras Ediciones, 2018).

59. Tapia, *Dialectica del Colonialism Interno*, 149.

apply the strategy and tactics of the Kurdish women's army when theorizing armed struggle? These are questions for which we still do not have answers, and for which we do not desire to have either: it will be the pueblo and peoples who rebel who are in charge of naming them, since it is the group that does the naming that forms part of the process of decolonization.

It would be a serious mistake, colonial and patriarchal in nature, to think that this new practice will be presented in the same format as the old political culture, which is currently in crisis. We should not believe that emancipatory processes aspire to defeat and overthrow the capitalist/state civilization in order to impose hegemony on society as a whole. The conflict between these two processes is not and cannot be symmetrical to the class struggle since it responds to distinct fundamental logics. The victory of the working class in the communist revolution would be, according to Marx, the end of wage labor and therefore the eradication of the proletariat. Across much of his works, Marx defends the thesis that the working class needs to become a ruling class in order to suppress the old relations of production. In *The Communist Manifesto*, he stresses that the aim is also to suppress "the conditions for the existence of class antagonisms and of classes generally and will thereby have abolished its own supremacy as a class." In other works, he was even clearer: "The history of all past society has consisted in the development of class antagonisms, antagonisms that assumed different forms at different epochs . . . one fact is common to all past ages, viz., the exploitation of one part of society by the other. . . . The Communist revolution is the most radical rupture with traditional property relations."[60] On the contrary, pueblos are rebelling to remain pueblos, to preserve themselves as such by

---

60. Karl Marx and Frederick Engels, "Manifesto of the Communist Party," in *Selected Works*, Vol.1 (Moscow: Progress Publishers, 1969), 125–26.

transforming themselves in their movement. The people struggle to recover and maintain their traditional ways and means of life, transforming them because, as I stated earlier, it is not a question of simply restoring what previously existed. The last thing they want is for the "dissolution of the old conditions of existence."[61]

In updating modes of existence, I find several processes unfolding: one is filtering through traditions to maintain only those that do not oppress other people, as patriarchy does; another is identifying the customs or ways of doing that have emancipatory potential (such as the minga/tequio) to generalize or scale them up once freed from their archaic bonds.

There is no possible symmetry here with class struggle, something that traditional leftist movements have yet to understand, just as they cannot accept that the feminist logics of collective care is a basic form of doing politics. For an example of this we can look at how poorly received the Zapatistas' decision to run a candidate for the Mexican presidency was by the left broadly defined. In May of 2017, María de Jesús Patricio Martínez, also known as Marichuy, was selected by the National Indigenous Congress of Mexico and the EZLN as a candidate for the presidency. Many people close to Zapatismo thought that it was just another electoral campaign, like those carried out by the traditional political parties, without understanding that there were *other* objectives, *other* modes, and ultimately, *other* ways of walking.

To confine the resistance of the pueblos in the framework of class struggle is a colonialist theoretical-political attitude. It ends up imposing upon them, from outside and from above, objectives and modes that they have not themselves chosen. Pueblos have other ways of doing politics and organizing, other temporalities and ways, because their objective is to remain a people, which they must in

---

61.   Marx and Engels, "Manifesto of the Communist Party," 125.

order to fight and get rid of capitalism, colonialism, and patriarchy. The organizations that considered themselves the vanguard needed to build a social base of "masses" to lead them, providing themselves with a leadership that, in the words of a Sandinista commander, "directed and determined the whole movement." Thus, the Sandinista National Liberation Front (FSLN) "was set to the monumental task of building, from its own apparatus, the organizational and revolutionary movement of the masses."[62] The apparatus commanded, and the people obeyed.

As extractivism—one of the main and most enduring features of colonialism—deepens, we can say that we are facing a neocolonial regime that reproduces the history of society and imposes itself upon another: in this case, it is a particular alliance between the large multinationals and sectors of the middle classes of the North and the South, which oppress all the societies from below. This reality should lead us to see the anticolonial and antipatriarchal strategies of these societies in movement as necessary inspirations for all oppressed societies.

The emancipatory path cannot consist of taking state power to impose a hegemony upon others, this would consummate their self-destruction, reproducing the dynamic of master and slave. These societies in movement are proceeding differently. Just as the original peoples of Latin America have been resisting the five centuries of colonialism, they are keeping the enemy at bay in order to sustain and reproduce the "radical otherness" of their own world.[63]

62. Jaime Wheelock and Marta Harnecker, *Vanguardia y Revolución En Las Sociedades Periféricas* (Madrid: Siglo Ventiuno Editores, 1986).

63. Raúl Zibechi, "La Radical Otredad," prologue to Pablo Albarenga, *Retomada* (Montevideo: Alter Ediciones, 2019).

Challenging Critical Thought from Below

The emergence of a new feminist/antipatriarchal wave, along with the ongoing historical anticolonial struggle of original peoples, demonstrate the limits of critical theory, in part due to its Western, Euro, and state-centric frameworks. Ever since the fall of the Berlin Wall and institutionalized socialism, left critical thought has wandered between reaffirming its accepted and established concepts, and searching new horizons. All of this has been happening with scant attention paid to the ongoing civilizational crisis, or the failure to find solutions to global crises. More so, left critical thought has been unable to provide a novel articulate analysis of these renewed anticolonial and antipatriarchal waves.

Antisystemic movements are certainly not the only actors that lay bare the limits of critical thought. The environmental crisis, climate chaos, and the civilizational crisis—entangled and closely linked processes—call into question some of the basic assumptions of the emancipatory theoretical framework. This framework is often anchored in economic centrality, models of development, and a concept of progress that has been widely criticized since Walter Benjamin's writing, but that still remains difficult to overcome.[1]

1.   Walter Benjamin, "Theses on the Philosophy of History," in *Critical Theory and Society: A Reader*, eds. Stephen Bronner and Douglas Kellner (London: Routledge, 2020).

In this sense, it is worth noting the powerful and unrelenting influence that some of the ideas of the leftist and progressive intelligentsia have maintained, despite decades of debate and their ostensible record of leading humanity to collapse. The very concept of revolution, as Bolívar Echeverría argues, "when speaking on Benjamin, must not be sacrificed for the sake of a promising future, but must contemplate a dimension that opens up toward the past."[2]

Concepts such as good living/living well (*sumak kawsay/ suma qamaña*) from the Andes, are beginning to take the place that revolutionary concepts once had, like "mode of production" for example.[3] This epistemic turn arises from a realization that concepts that were created to account for a concrete reality should not be extended into completely different worlds, as Pierre Clastres argued in his polemic with Marxist anthropologists.[4] Similarly, antipatriarchal and feminist theorization—out of Latin America, Kurdistan, and other regions—that centralizes the reproduction of life is displacing the all-encompassing role that Marx-inspired social science had granted to the working-class subject, given the important role it believed it held in productivity.[5]

We can similarly reflect upon concepts such as structure and superstructure, dictatorship of the proletariat and the general idea of socialism. These are all concepts that have been left behind,

---

2. Bolívar Echeverría, *Siete Aproximaciones a Walter Benjamin* (Bogotá: Desde Abajo, 2010), 41.

3. A concept from Andean cosmology—*sumaq kawsay* (Quechua) or *suma qamaña* (Aymara)—has been scaled up and adopted in different ways as a guiding principle of good governance, albeit not without controversy. Loosely translating to *plentiful life*, they have been used in part to grant rights to Pachamama or Mother Earth in Ecuador and Bolivia's constitutions.

4. Pierre Clastres, *Society Against the State: Essays in Political Anthropology* (Princeton: Princeton University Press, 2020).

5. Silvia Federici, "The Unfinished Feminist Revolution," *The Commoner* 15 (Winter 2012).

no longer occupying a central place in critical thought, or if they are, they have been completely reconceptualized as in the case of "socialism of the twenty-first century."[6]

In what follows, I investigate the limitations of critical thought in the West while also thinking through ways around these limitations, arguing that they no longer inspire emancipatory movements in the face of growing global tensions. These limits are exacerbated by the civilizational crisis, which operates by neutralizing the traditional modes of knowledge anchored in the subject-object colonial relationship.[7]

Between the Universal and the Particular

American sociologist Immanuel Wallerstein argues that the most important challenges facing the social sciences are nestled in Eurocentrism and colonialism, leaving behind the different concepts of social time, rationality, and modernity.[8] Although I agree with the first two aspects that Wallerstein mentions—to which others may be added—which are closely intertwined, I proceed by examining them separately to deepen my analysis.

Despite important criticism and partial setbacks, the claim to universality found in the social sciences and critical thought remains hegemonic. Although Eurocentrism seems to be a topical issue, the critique of hegemonic politics can be traced backed to the

---

6. "Socialism of the twenty-first century" is the term used to describe the governing models put into place by leftists in Latin America at the turn of the last century. Many of these governments were also collectively described as the "Pink Tide" in the media.

7. Linda Tuhiwai Smith, *Decolonizing Methodologies: Research and Indigenous Peoples* (New York: Bloomsbury Publishing, 2021).

8. Immanuel Wallerstein, *Unthinking Social Science: The Limits of Nineteenth-Century Paradigms* (Philadelphia: Temple University Press, 2001).

1950s, when Aimé Césaire resigned from the French Communist Party in his famous letter to its secretary general, Maurice Thorez. We could even go back to the 1930s, when Mao Zedong turned his back on one of the key declarations of the Third International for China, announcing that the driving force of the revolution in his country was not the working class but the peasantry.

Césaire drafted his letter of resignation in 1956, the year First Secretary of the Communist Party Nikita Khrushchev submitted his report to the twentieth Congress, in which he denounced Stalin's crimes, including his cruel repression of the Hungarian uprising. Césaire reveals "shock, pain and shame" at the events mentioned, but also at the passivity of the French party and, most importantly, the way that it focuses on the struggle of colonized peoples for their liberation.[9] "The colonial question," he writes, "cannot be treated as a part of a more important whole."[10]

Note the similarity to the proposals put forth by feminist movements, which in those years were told to postpone their demands until the triumph of the revolution. Against the hegemonic currents of the left and in general critical thought, Césaire considered that the struggle against racism by peoples of color to be more complex than that of the French workers' struggle against capitalism. He denounced what he considered "colonialist paternalism," a conception in vogue in the first half of the twentieth century, which distinguished between "advanced" and "backward" peoples, in an exact replica of colonialist thought. It was this thesis that led the international left to believe that it should be the advanced societies that should lead the socialist path.

I think it is important to highlight two aspects of this luminous text. The first refers to the type of organization that the communists

---

9.   Aimé Césaire, "Letter to Maurice Thorez," *Social Text* 28, no. 2 (2010): 145.

10.   Césaire, "Letter to Maurice Thorez," 147.

proposed, centered on the elevation of a small group of people to a position of power in a hierarchical and authoritarian organization. Césaire proposed the opposite: an organization as broad and flexible as possible, "capable of giving impetus to the greatest number (rather than ordering around a small number)," in which revolutionaries should play "their role of leavening, inspiring, and orienting."[11] In fact, I would argue he is proposing community-inspired, non-avant-garde spaces where peasants will create organizations "by them, and adapted to ends that they alone can determine."[12]

Although he does not directly mention it, Césaire alludes to the self-organization of Black peoples. Later on, his pupil, Frantz Fanon in *The Wretched of the Earth*, would express it more directly when he denounced the same party for limiting itself to working in Algeria with the elite urban workers and civil servants, a group that barely made up 1 percent of the population, all the while despising the peasant masses and dismissing activism in rural areas. Contrary to the political conceptualization of the vanguard and elite that seeks to lead the peoples from outside and from above, Césaire bets on the development of the peoples "by means of internal growth, interior necessity, and organic progress, without anything exterior coming to warp, alter, or compromise this growth.."[13] In my view, this is how the women's and Indigenous peoples' movements in Latin America have been expanding in recent decades.

The second issue Césaire's letter addresses is the relationship between the universal and the particular, rejecting the communist notion of peoples (women could also be added in this period) as mere pieces of a global strategy. Césaire's letter refuses to either bury itself in a narrow particularism, what can be read as a kind of cultural relativism and in "a disembodied universalism" that effaces

---

11.   Césaire, "Letter to Maurice Thorez," 148.
12.   Césaire, "Letter to Maurice Thorez," 148.
13.   Césaire, "Letter to Maurice Thorez," 149.

difference for the sake of building a totality. He argues that the left can be lost both in closing itself in the particular and by dissolving into the universal. As Wallerstein points out, the left has been debating since then about "how to configure a form of universalism constituted by a deepening of multiple particularities."[14] This debate is far from settled and is at the heart of the crisis of critical thought that we are currently experiencing.

I return here to the work of the Egyptian sociologist Anouar Abdel-Malek, whose work *Social Dialectics*, I cited earlier. Abdel-Malek highlights the temporality of ideas and their limitation in time and space: "How can one imagine a universalism that is itself contingent, marked by historical necessity and historically determined as a world view?"[15] A fierce pioneering critic of Orientalism, Abdel-Malek "defended the thesis that Orientalism and colonization went hand in hand in the colonial adventure."[16] But he was not satisfied with denunciation either, as he also investigated the ways to overcome colonialism and imperialism. To get out of the universalist abstraction, Abdel-Malek studies the "historical specificity" of oppressed nations, by dividing the world into two civilizations or "outer circles" (the Chinese and the Indo-Aryan) and multiple cultural areas or "intermediate circles." Abdel-Malek contends that "there is no universal without comparisons," and focuses on the dialectic of the specific that allows him to delve into the differences and particularities that are part of the universal.[17]

14. Immanuel Wallerstein, "Aimé Césaire: Colonialismo, Comunismo y Negritud," in *Discurso Sobre El Colonialismo* (Madrid: Ediciones Akal, 2006).

15. Anouar Abdel-Malek, *Social Dialectics*, Vol. 1, *Civilisations and Social Theory* (London: Macmillan Press, 1981), 4.

16. Bernabé López García, "Anouar Abdel-Malek, Sociólogo Egipcio," *El País*, June 25, 2012, https://elpais.com/cultura/2012/06/25/actualidad/1340658925_424955.html.

17. García, "Anouar Abdel-Malek."

In this framework, Abdel-Malek points to the limits of Marxism as a "general sociological conception": "The application of this method to the advanced industrial societies will not yield up any lasting contribution to the non-Western societies in their hour of renaissance."[18] Abdel-Malek writes in the years of Vietnam's victorious resistance to the invasion by the United States and the Chinese Cultural Revolution, when it broke away from Soviet socialism. However, if Marxism were applied, he argues, "from the principle of historical specificity," it would be a great help in the understanding of non-Western civilizations. He formulates the limits of the theory of imperialism as it was spreading in the 1960s because it was detached from national movements: "If we look at the so-called scientific studies of imperialism, it is clear that the ideas of those movements engaged for the last century and a half in a struggle against colonialism (or archaeo-imperialism) and imperialism are practically ignored. Absent too, though perhaps not entirely so, are the ideas of those mass workers' movements whose struggles are usually considered by orthodox thought to have been immobilized."[19]

Let us remember that in those years imperialism was basically analyzed as an economic and political-military phenomenon. Consequently, any denunciation of the misdeeds of the West in the Third World was only done with an inverted Eurocentric gaze, in which oppressed peoples were condemned to the role of victims and therefore were seen as incapable of emancipating themselves.[20]

According to Abel-Malek, it is not possible to understand imperialism (or colonialism, and I would also add patriarchy) without taking as a starting point the conflict with nationalist and

---

18. Abdel-Malek, *Social Dialectics*, Vol. 1, 117.
19. Anouar Abdel-Malek, *Social Dialectics*, Vol. 2, *Nation and Revolution* (London: Macmillan Press, 1981), 116.
20. Mary Louise Pratt, *Imperial Eyes: Travel Writing and Transculturation* (London: Routledge, 2007).

feminist movements. To limit oneself to the analysis of accumulation, of the primacy of finance capital and monopolies, of the export of capital and of the interests of the military-industrial complex, implies sacrificing those who resist upon the altar of universalism, or reducing them to mere objects of analysis: "Imperialism has existed only as long as there have been nations, national formations, and national movements that aspired to independence and autonomy, an autonomy that colonialism and later imperialism have seen it as their mission to hold back, subjugate, dismantle and destroy."[21] At this point, his gaze focused on conflict and not on structure, here in dialogue with the thought of the historian E. P. Thompson, who in those same years avoided the abstract and universalist schemes detached from Soviet Marxism most notably in his *The Making of the English Working Class*.

Finally, I would like to highlight the challenges and perhaps issues in Abdel-Malek's comparative analysis, particularly as it concerns the heterogeneity of Latin America. He is unable to fully close his analysis, in particular when he is forced to divide the region into an Indo-European cultural area (yet related to Africa) in which he includes regions with Black majorities such as Brazil and the Caribbean but fails to include Indigenous peoples in either of the two civilizations he describes.

This challenge brings us back to one of the main characteristics of the Latin American region: its historical-structural heterogeneity.[22] Critical theory finds here one of its greatest limits, which derives from the difficulty of and inability to think and elaborate concepts from the historical experience and reality of pueblos, instead of generalizing and imposing ideas and concepts elaborated in the global North.

---

21. Abdel-Malek, *Social Dialectics*, Vol. 2, 133.
22. Aníbal Quijano, "Coloniality of Power and Eurocentrism in Latin America," *International Sociology* 15, no. 2 (June 2000): 215–32.

The Critical Thought of Indigeneity

Over the last few decades, the most original contributions to critical thought have come from the experiences and cosmovision of Indigenous peoples. As an introduction to this claim, I would like to draw a bridge between the *Amautic* thought of the Aymara theorist Fausto Reinaga and the ideas expressed by the Insurgent Subcomandante Moisés in their seminar "Critical Thinking in the Face of the Capitalist Hydra."[23]

As Bolivian writer Esteban Ticona points out, "Reinaga is not an intellectual who draws from theory to interpret the Bolivian reality and the world; he is a thinker who learned to interpret reality from the praxis of life," a practice that connects him with thinkers like Fanon, among others.[24] Anchoring his theorization in his life experiences allows him to cross the boundaries between currents of thought and academic disciplines, unrestricted from its rigid borders. But most importantly, Reinaga's organic theorization allows him to address global problems, particularly colonization, from an Aymara-Indigenous perspective.

A notable process of Reinaga's thinking is his transition from Indigenous to *Amautic* thought, without having to mention Marxist-Leninist thought. In this process, the Tiwanaku Manifesto, issued in 1973 by four Indigenous organizations "at the foot of the great Inca stones of Tiwanaku," was disseminated clandestinely in Spanish, Quechua, and Aymara and used as a text for the formation of cadres in the midst of the dictatorship of Hugo Bánzer (1971–1978), and this moment quickly becomes the beginning of "the

---

23. An *Amauta* refers to a wise person, teacher, or philosopher in the Andes. The meeting was held May 2–9, 2015, in Chiapas.
24. Esteban Ticona, "El Indianismo de Fausto Reinaga: Orígenes, Desarrollo y Experiencia En Qullasuyo Bolivia," (PhD diss, Universidad Andina Simón Bolívar, 2015), 103.

cultural, political and economic decolonization of the country."[25] Here we find a new Indigenous consciousness, one that though it does relate to the national revolution of 1952, most importantly is responding to the continuity of the colonial situation, linking the "long memory" of anticolonial struggles with the "short memory" of the peasant and mining struggles around 1952, as the Bolivian theorist Silvia Rivera points out.

The Tiwanaku Manifesto and the birth of the Katarist current forged in the paths made by Indianism was made possible by the success of the 1952 revolution in the areas of education and political participation, which opened spaces for peasants and Indians, but also by its unfinished liberal project.[26] The Indian/Indigenous is, for Reinaga, the oppressed nation, a human collective that fights for its liberation. It is not dependent upon skin color but rather close relationships with nature and life, and also a nation/people who carry a culture, a religion and a philosophy. Hence, for Reinaga, Indianism is the spirit and organization capable of channeling the Indian/Indigenous revolution against the oppressors.

Reinaga's ideas are driven by a will to liberate an oppressed people. His *Amautic* thought (Andean wisdom) starts from this position, seeking to deepen the relationship of original peoples with nature, questioning the centrality of the human over all else, in order to open up to a cosmic conception of the universe and life. In that sense, "Reinaga is the main precursor of what is now called 'good living'" in Latin American critical discourse.[27]

In the interest of critical dialogue, I would like to highlight some important aspects of *Amautic* thought to bring it together

---

25. Ticona, "El Indianismo de Fausto Reinaga," 117.
26. Ticona, "El Indianismo de Fausto Reinaga," 121. "Indianism" captures the broader revival movements of Indigenous thought found at different historical moments across Latin America.
27. Ticona, "El Indianismo de Fausto Reinaga," 136.

with Zapatismo. In *Amautic* thought, time is conceptualized as circular; Indigenous peoples think and feel as a community, with the collective goal not being progress but to establish a different relationship with the past. In Reinaga's words, *Amautic* thought is premised on a "return to the path" or "enter[ing] the road."[28] It is worth emphasizing that it is not a theory but a reading of one's own experience, both as individual and collective.

Insurgente Comandante Moisés in his address "Political Economy from the Zapatista Communities I and II," at the "Critical Thinking in the Face of the Capitalist Hydra" seminar, reflects on the economy of the communities. He outlines two keys parts of Zapatismo from the start: the recovered land (which he calls "Mother Earth") and collective work, which are always intertwined and inseparable aspects of Zapatista identity.[29] Seeking ever more riches, colonialism and capitalism forced them off their ancestral lands, and over three decades, they had to invent ways to survive the State's attempts to take control and dispossess them of their reclaimed land.

As mentioned in the introduction, collective practice is the core of the Zapatista movement and, I would say, of any movement that includes Indigenous peoples, under diverse place-based names throughout the region. Collective or communal work is the backbone of the life of Indigenous peoples.

Like the production and reproduction of life, self-governance or autonomy is cyclical, moving around the collective work of peoples, municipalities, and regions, making it diverse and decentralized like the communities themselves. Although collective work includes all the people who make up the movement, its modes,

---

28.   Ticona, "El Indianismo de Fausto Reinaga," 141.
29.   Subcomandante Insurgente Moisés, "Political Economy from the Zapatista Communities I," in *Critical Thought in the Face of the Capitalist Hydra I* (Durham, NC: Paper Boat Press, 2016).

schedules, and characteristics are defined autonomously in each unique place. In agreement with what Guatemalan scholar and thinker Tzul Tzul proposes, Moisés emphasizes that collective work has allowed them to "monitor our government," because they are the ones who administer, the junta of good government, or the MAREZ.[30]

Based on the commentary above, I propose some ideas as bridges between Fausto Reinaga and Subcomandante Moisés's ways of looking at the world, which could be extended to the experiences of other Indigenous peoples, such as the reflections embodied by Indigenous thinkers like Lorenzo Muelas of the Nasa community, Mixe scholar Floriberto Díaz, and Kichwa Luis Macas, among many others.

To start, while both Moisés and Reinaga reflect on their life experiences, they do not do so by bringing theories "down" from books and into their reality. Moisés and Reinaga work to systematize in struggle what pueblos are doing in order to reproduce themselves as such.

At this point there are two key issues to consider. One is that reflecting on one's own experience is not intended for a codification as "theory," nor does it seek universal recognition. Two, it is a kind of reflection turned inward toward collective experiences. This type of reflection breaks from the traditional relationship of researcher (or leader) and researched (or bases), as these reflections instead seek to strengthen the community network in what could be defined as "decolonization of methodologies."[31]

Both Moisés and Reinaga also center Mother Earth, the hills and rivers, skies and plants. Here we find multiple subjects with

---

30. Subcomandante Insurgente Moisés, "Resistance and Rebellion III," in *Critical Thought*, 138.

31. Tuhiwai, *Decolonizing Methodologies* (New York: Bloomsbury Publishing, 2021).

whom the people interact in a relationship of interiority, the only way possible communities find in order to maintain a balanced relationship with what the West calls "nature." Louise Pratt reminds us that the classification system of the natural world created by the West in the eighteenth century "created the task of locating every species on the planet, extracting it from its particular, arbitrary surroundings (the chaos), and placing it in its appropriate spot in the system (the order-book, collection, or garden) with its new written, secular European name."[32]

It is worth remembering that the systematization of nature and thought occurred simultaneously with slavery in the West and the system of plantations and the genocide of Indigenous peoples. Strictly speaking, it is not so much that they coincide but rather are the material basis that made both systematizations possible. In hindsight, we can come to understand how slavery, monocultures, and genocides were "massive experiments in social engineering and discipline, serial production, the systematization of human life, the standardizing of persons."[33] Slave rebellions and insurrections by native peoples interrupt this process of systematization, subjection, and control of life, and also the work of researchers and scientists. As much as the scientists are unsettled by the reminder, "the term 'research' is intrinsically linked to European Imperialism and colonialism," being one of the "dirtiest words in the Indigenous world's vocabulary."[34] Perhaps it for this reason that the thoughts and feelings of the world's oppressed peoples have been so difficult to recognize as authentic knowledges by academia and critical thought.

The third element these scholars who reflect "from below" share is the centrality of community: the *ayllu* as identity for Reinaga and

---

32. Pratt, *Imperial Eyes*, 31.
33. Pratt, *Imperial Eyes*, 36.
34. Smith, *Decolonizing Methodologies*, 1.

collective work for Moisés.[35] The community is not an institution endowed with collective lands, families, and authorities elected in assemblies, nor can it be limited to the existence of community commons. The community is made up of the collective practices carried out to ensure the reproduction of life, informed by a belief that, done independently, the reproduction of life would not be possible.[36] The most prominent struggle today is between life (and its reproduction) and the objectification/abstraction of social relations. Given the materialist essence of the State, the adoption of good living (*buen vivir*) has been misinterpreted as revolving around having more objects or generalizing the collective ownership of things.

Challenging Neoliberal Feminism from the Grassroots

Half a century has passed since the global revolution of 1968, the epicenter of which was the universities of Paris and other countries of the North and South, where young people questioned the authoritarianism of the academies. Feminist struggles in the universities have shown that little has changed since, as the number of harassment complaints, cases of violence and discrimination carries on in spaces where it was thought asymmetrical gender relations had improved. In spite of all of this, some things have changed.

Feminist thought and practices have disrupted the culture that revolved around the idea of a vanguard, both in politics and art, posing serious questions with regards to academic ways of knowing and researching that depend on the subject-object relationship.

---

35. An *Ayllu* is an Andean community composed of elements beyond the human, including the territories, nonhuman relatives such as the rivers and *Apus* (mountain spirits), and other *pachas* or times.

36. Raúl Zibechi, "Los Trabajos Colectivos Como Bienes Comunes Material/Simbólicos," *El Apantle* 1 (October 2015).

Feminists have led the charge in questioning hierarchical structures, from churches to political parties. At this point it is clear that it has not just been organized women who have had the most profound impact on political cultures, as their criticisms of patriarchy have had far-reaching consequences.

Since 2017, a march called Alerta Feminista (Feminist Alert) has been held every time a woman is murdered in the city of Montevideo, Uruguay. The marches bring together between two hundred and two thousand women, and a handful of men who walk at the end or to the sides of the march. It is a combative march with radical cries against patriarchy, sexist violence, and the State. One of the most powerful aspects of the march is the collective reading of a text that is distributed at it.[37] They have dispensed with the classic scene, of a speaker amplified by a sound car, typically found at union and party demonstrations.

The organizers, belonging to the Coordinadora de Feminismos (a local feminist collective), argue that the shout and response format done collectively is one of the most important features of the movement's street actions. They believe that this way of doing implies "a decentralization of the interlocutor," since they speak to themselves, distance themselves from representative and state-centric politics, and construct a "constellation of voices" in which both the most active and those who only attend the marches participate, breaking the dichotomy between those who speak and those who listen, between the militants and the followers of the movement.[38]

On the last two International Women's Days, a debate has been held between women of the Coordinadora de Feminismos and

37. Victoria Furtado Alonzo and Valeria Grabino Etorena, "Alertas Feministas: Lenguajes y Estéticas de Un Feminismo Desde El Sur," in *Momento de Paro, Tiempo de Rebelion: Miradas Feministas Para Reinventar la Lucha* (Montevideo: Minervas Ediciones, 2018), 105.
38. Furtado and Grabino, "Alertas Feministas," 106.

institutional feminists. The latter, in agreement with the affiliates of the trade union center, defended having a speaker on a platform, who reads a text agreed upon by the conveners. After extensive and intense debates, the women's' organizations that centered traditional political cultures, such as Cotidiano Mujer and Intersocial, were overwhelmed by the activism of the younger feminists. It was the young radicals who argued that placing a speaker at top of a platform is a way of reproducing patriarchal cultures. It was a clear victory for young radical women, in what can be interpreted as an extraordinary change in political culture. However, this is not to imply that things cannot revert.

In her last publication, *Reflexiones en Torno Ideas y Prácticas del Entre-Mujeres a Principios del Siglo XXI*, the late Italian Mexican feminist Francesca Gargallo analyzed the tense relations between young university feminists and academic authorities and male students. She argues that, in addition to denouncing the violence and harassment of teachers in the academy, they no longer find incentive in competition or in gaining equality with men. Rather, these women tend toward autonomous and collective intellectual production that they often carry out outside the universities, manifesting a rejection of authorship, so revered by academic patriarchs.[39]

A notable aspect of this work is the understanding of how relations between different generations of feminists are changing. According to Gargallo, in the context of growing femicidal violence, many young university students show a critical attitude toward university gender studies and the contents of these courses, while maintaining tense relations with the "specialists" in gender studies who work in academia. This new generation refuses to abide by the recommendations of the most experienced feminists, whom they

---

39. Francesca Gargallo, *Reflexiones En Torno a Ideas y Prácticas del Entre-Mujeres a Principios del Siglo XXI* (Bogotá: Desde Abajo, 2019).

consider "sacred cows" (recognized professors and authors), who in turn have little or no practice in the streets nor any participatory experience in grassroot collectives. As anti-neoliberal feminists, many young university students are opting for collective intellectual and artistic creation and the expression of their emotions and feelings, rather than going through the individual and institutional path to develop as professionals.

Even the forms their denunciation of misogynistic and sexist professors takes teaches vitality and unprecedented methods: they seize classrooms and spaces of power in universities, cover their faces to denounce aggressors, and open separatist spaces that do not respond "to the demand for their own space for women's self-awareness, as was the case in the 1970s but rather as safe spaces so as to not to be attacked, questioned, and ridiculed."[40]

I noted similar processes, although of a different character, in the three visits to peasant and Indigenous communities I carried out in early 2022: in Temuco (South of Chile), in Blanco (Cuenca, Ecuador) and in San Francisco Echeverría (El Salvador). In Temuco, the new role of Mapuche women is notable in three very different areas: in the communication collective Mapuexpress, among market vendors who defy prohibition and persecution from street vending, and among the academics of Austral University who make up the Mapuche History Collective.[41]

San Francisco Echeverría in El Salvador is a town of just over a thousand inhabitants. Peasant families attempted to repopulate the town after the internal conflict of the 1980s had devastated many prominently Indigenous communities. The vast majority

40. Francesca Gargallo Celentani, *Reflexiones En Torno* (Bogotá: Ediciones Desde Abajo, 2019).
41. Raúl Zibechi, "El Colonialismo se Estrella con las Mujeres Mapuche," *La Jornada*, August 16, 2019, https://www.jornada.com.mx/2019/08/16/opinion/018a2pol.

of the members of the Community Development Association are women, who make up the majority of its committees and are those who promote activities that improve the life of the community, such as the promotion of worker cooperatives, urban cleaning, the maintenance of the community library, and the denunciation of the use of agrochemicals in the corn crops of local peasants, all who are former guerrilla combatants.

The most notable case of a decentralized feminism is perhaps Ecuador, where women not only play a central role in resistance to mining, a fact recognized and respected by the men of their communities, they have also organized a collective called Women's Front for the Defense of Mother Earth (Frente de Mujeres Defensoras de la Pachamama, popularly named "pachamamas"), a frontline organization for the care and defense of life and Mother Earth. This collective was created by midwives from the parish of Molleturo (Macizo de Cajas, Cuenca), where more than thirty communities are resisting mining, and came together to burn down the campsite of the Chinese Ecuagoldmining company on May 8, 2018.[42] In fact, the Women's Front for the Defense of Mother Earth was created in 2008 by peasants and Indigenous people whose participation "can be explained by the role their families and communities hold as guardians of the needs and interests of reproduction, which are directly affected or put at risk with the development of the mine."[43]

Sociologist Lina Solano understands that the social position of these women allows them to have a greater understanding of the priorities for the survival of families and have, among other

42. Raúl Zibechi, "Defensoras de la Pachamama," *Rebelión*, March 31, 2021, https://rebelion.org/defensoras-de-la-pachamama.
43. Lina Magali Solano Ortiz, "Impactos Sociales de La Minería a Gran Escala En La Fase de Exploración y El Rol de Las Defensoras de La Pachamama En La Resistencia a Los Proyectos Río Blanco y Quimsacocha" (Master's Thesis, Universidad de Cuenca, 2013), 59.

qualities, close and affective contact with the water being polluted by mining companies. Indeed, their dual role as mothers and midwives allows them to understand the urgencies imposed on them by their defense of life: "When the water sources are affected, they must travel long distances to stock up, which increases their workload."[44] In addition, mining companies only employ women for cleaning and cooking at the mines. Researching for her master's thesis, Solano collected testimonies from native women about police persecutions and prosecutions. She spoke with the pachamamas and the Front of Women Guardians of the Amazon, almost all of whom had very little previous organizational experience. "Our childhood was the water, most importantly it was the river's running water," recalls Francisca.[45] "It was wonderful . . . we drank water from the wells, we went to bathe in the river, we used to take the river's water with us in pitchers . . . it was a very beautiful life," exclaims Isaura, seventy-two. Both women are from rural the communities of Tarqui and Victoria de Portete.[46]

When we city dwellers say, "water is life," we formulate an abstract slogan, like so many others. For the *comuneras* (community folk), on the other hand, it is life itself. Water is the subject of their lives, like the moor and snowy peaks, plants and animals. Perhaps that is why collective leaderships form on their own, like springs, passing through the side of egos and protagonists, so typical of the world of men. At this point, I must point out that the pachamamas are mostly midwives, which gives them a place of respect and moral autonomy in their communities, as I have witnessed in San Pedro de Yumate, Ecuador, where the community prevents the passage of trucks and machinery from the mining company.[47]

---

44. Solano Ortiz, "Impactos Sociales," 63.
45. Solano Ortiz, "Impactos Sociales," 70.
46. Solano Ortiz, "Impactos Sociales," 119–20.
47. Zibechi, "Defensoras de la Pachamama."

Recap

A civilizational crisis occurs when new problems cannot be solved with the resources available for that civilization. Critical thinking emerged in the north of the planet, closely linked to the French and Russian revolutions, and was partially a response to the experiences of the Paris Commune and to the Labor and socialist movements of the nineteenth and early twentieth centuries. A good portion of the terms that were conceptualized in this period, from *revolution* to *tabula rasa* (a term from the Enlightenment, meaning the human is devoid of any innate knowledge), cannot simply be transplanted to other parts of the world. To uncritically carry over concepts born from and as a consequence of colonial encounters can serve to produce neocolonial practices.

In the current moment of systemic and civilizational crisis, we have in Latin America the urgent need to be inspired by feminist movements and Indigenous peoples, as we try to overcome the limitations of Eurocentrism put in place in critical thinking: women have presented nonpatriarchal ways of doing politics, which have in the modes of reproduction, their starting point and inspiration.[48] Indigenous peoples, meanwhile, emphasize that the community, anchored in communal work, is the way of life that allows both an anticapitalist resistance and the creation of new worlds.

When the feminisms from below and the movements of Indigenous communities come together, as is currently happening through the whirlwind of this civilizational crisis, everything is possible. A thousand ideas flourish, the most diverse ways of doing

---

48. Raquel Gutiérrez Aguilar, "A Propósito del Trabajo de Silvia Federici: Colocar la Reproducción Material y Simbólica de la Vida Social y la Capacidad Humana de Producir Lo Común Como Punto de Partida Para la Reflexión Crítica y la Práctica Política," *El Apantle* 1 (October 2015): 169–76.

things begin to unfold, realities are interwoven with the most unsuspecting dreams, those that allow us to glimpse at other worlds and realize that their manifestation only depends on those of us committed to its creation.

Betting on Diversity Means Rejecting Unity and Homogenization

Question (Q): We would like to talk about your political horizons.[1] What brought you to where you are today; what events changed your foundational beliefs? What would you say were the turning points that placed you on your current trajectory as a militant? Is it possible to think of ways of knowing and researching that are separate from one's own ways of doing politics, from the modes of existence in the struggle?

Answer (A): There were perhaps two or three turning points in my life. During my exile in Spain in the seventies, I came to encounter the first feminist wave.[2] The truth is that coming from Latin America, that was a hard blow to the revolutionary male ego and my first reaction was defensive. Despite the impact, I managed to question my way of thinking, which at the time was linked to Marxism and Leninism. As I look back, I am now able to recognize

---

1.   This interview was conducted by Alana Moraes, Lucas Keese, and Marcelo Hotimsky of Editora Elefante in São Paolo, Brazil on June 24, 2020. It originally appeared in Raúl Zibechi, *Territórios em Rebeldia* (São Paolo: Editora Elefante, 2022).

2.   The author is speaking of the global feminist movement, hence noting the 1970s as part of the first wave.

how feminism was progressively unsettling my convictions about how I understood power, the State, the party, and revolution.

The second influential turn came from Zapatismo. For years I had been learning about Indigenous communities in the Andean region, deeply impacted by them as well as *Indigenista* writers such as José María Arguedas and some Peruvian thinkers like Alberto Flores Galindo. But Zapatismo was fundamental for me, as it had an impact on my politics and thought, and not to mention having an affective impact as well. Living with communities and support bases changes the way you see the world, the way you see yourself, and calls into question the ways of thinking and doing.

Perhaps there is a third, more recent turning point, but I think it is still too early to understand it in depth. It is related to the crisis of progressivism that has emerged since at least June 2013 with the governing crisis in Brazil but which also saw the emergence of the collective subjects from "below," such as the movements led by Black and Amazonian peoples in Brazil.[3] At some point I had trusted progressive governments, especially Lula's. He is considered by many as one of the first of the Pink Tide, but my enthusiasm was short-lived. So, June 2013 was and somehow still is something different, not so much because of the street protests that are always significant but for two additional reasons: it showed the limits of progressivism and leftism and taught that there are alternatives rooted in places beyond the State, working hand in hand with other subjects.

Young people, women, and *favelados* (people from the favelas) are playing a more important role than it seems. All of this has not yet been fully understood, but it is emerging at different moments from different places. Both the crisis of the left (from the Workers Party [PT] to the Landless Peasant Movement [MST]) and the

---

3. Here Zibechi refers to the mobilizations that began as a response to transit fare hikes in 2013, growing into widespread rebellions against austerity and state oppression in various sectors of society.

recomposition of the popular movements have become most evident during the COVID-19 pandemic.[4] In this sense, meeting militants in favelas such as Maré and Alemao, in Rio, filled me with questions and led me down different paths, from the work of Abdias do Nascimento to the role of theater and music in the formation of Black collective subjects.[5]

Along with the ruin of these left projects came the bankruptcy of other ways of knowing, thinking, and investigating from white leaders, academics, writers, and militants. At this point, revolutionary thought and practice was facing another reality: critical thinking ceased to be centered in writing, in the book, and became diversified in the productions that occurred in the popular world, from dance and rituality to acting and body movement. I want to say that my role as a white adult in revolutionary struggle was also questioned by the emergence of collective subjects, particularly feminists and the Black youth in Brazil. It was time to put things into perspective, and think, what's next?

As you can imagine, I do not have the answer. It would be too self-centered to think that I, as an individual, am going to have it from a Western urban frame of thinking. What I do know is that the answer can only come about through intense work, individual and collective work that is antipatriarchal, anticolonial, and anti-Eurocentric. All this means confronting the white male ego, killing it by rethinking our positions and ourselves, to work with others and, above all, those who are increasingly far from the center and in the margins. During this pandemic I have just been trying to be a thread that transmits what the pueblos are doing, because

4.   "The crisis of the left" refers to widespread sentiments held by activists in Latin America who note structural and systemic failures of governance since the rise of the so-called Pink Tide.

5.   Abdias do Nascimento was a notable Brazilian poet and scholar known for creating the Black Experimental Theater, and a critical Pan-African thinker.

they are the ones who teach us, and we are just their students. This is what the Zapatistas have been saying for years, but we have often dismissed it as simple rhetoric.

In short, we have to rethink ourselves. We need to question who the speaker is, their positionality, that is, the territories from which a speech is broadcast, and that means questioning ourselves, debating, and accepting that we are not the center of anything but only a hinge.

Q: Many important events have taken place in Latin America and the world [over the last few years]. The crisis of the so-called progressive governments consolidated at the same time with wins of far-right leaders who have relied upon great popular support. You highlight the question of the model of accumulation by dispossession or Fourth World War in Zapatista terms, political-economic modes present even in the progressive governments of the region.[6]

Can it be argued that far-right governments are more complete expressions of this extractivist project because they can bury the expectations of "social inclusion"? Or are we witnessing another kind of project underway? How do you understand the emergence of this scenario in the Latin American context, in the face of the so-called crisis of progressivism and what can the struggles for autonomy contribute at this time?

A: I think that extreme right-wing governments do not necessarily have a defined project but are probably the expression of the crisis, a response from the dominant and middle classes, but also from the institutions that feel that this crisis is something new and different that can do away with them. If our strategic projects have

6.   "The Fourth World War," a concept from the Zapatistas, refers to our current epoch of protracted institutionalized violence against the poor, which is perpetuated by the State.

been derailed by reality, we can think that something similar happens to the right. I believe that the only state institution that is still standing, and will continue for a long time, is the armed forces. It is no coincidence that in the midst of the crisis in Brazil, they have stepped forward and occupied key spaces of power.

My impression is that the ruling classes have only one project, which is to remain at the top, to remain dominant. The rest is improvised. Meanwhile, they appeal to the State to resolve the problems from below. It is a mistake to think that the economy and profit is paramount for them. Capitalism is not an economy—here I am following Abdullah Öcalan—it is a project of power, a type of power threaded around the domination of women, Indigenous, and Black peoples. Therefore, it is utopian to think that control of the State can be wrested from the ruling class, because the State itself is a tool created by the bourgeoisie to serve them.

So, I think the problem is found on our side: two centuries of state-centricity have led to the bankruptcy of emancipatory politics. This conclusion is based on experience, and has nothing to do with ideologies, nor with Marxism or with anarchism. But let's be honest: there is no ready-made alternative to replace a strategy anchored in the takeover of the State.

A bigger problem exists within critical thinking. I offer here for instance a comparative a look across the North and South. The accumulation that came about from an expanded reproduction of capital and industrial capitalism corresponded with a welfare state in the first world/Global North. In the global south we have not yet seen any comparable response to precarity. We must look at what type of state exists in a period of accumulation by dispossession in the South of the world and in the zones of nonbeing, those places where subjectivity and collectivity are not recognized.[7]

---

7.   "Zones of nonbeing" is a concept borrowed from Frantz Fanon.

That is where Zapatismo's concept of the Fourth World War comes into force. By this they mean a permanent war of dispossession to remove the population from their territories, to appropriate and redesign them according to the desire of the ruling class. This is what happens in areas where agribusiness is expanding in the Amazon, across mining and monocultures throughout the continent but also urban extractivism in large cities. The Olympics and the World Cup were the excuse to evict hundreds of thousands of people from their homes, as happened with Vila Autódromo in Río de Janeiro.

The kind of state that corresponds to this brutal form of accumulation cannot be democracy. The military occupation of the favelas, the war against the poor across the continent, is simply a politic of domination that makes dispossession possible. The left does not want to enter this debate and believes that if Bolsonaro falls it would be all "peace and love" again. Impossible. The broader left fails to understand that Brazil will not return to the FHC and the era of Lula unless there is a much more powerful popular revolt than there was in 2013.[8]

Q: Before the COVID-19 pandemic, South America was beginning to experience a new cycle of struggle against the neoliberal consensus in Colombia, Ecuador, and Chile. In the context of the crisis caused by the pandemic, there is a clear strengthening of the State as "protector" and administrator of body sovereignty. New surveillance and biosurveillance technologies seem to have gained legitimacy even within sectors that identify as progressive. In São Paulo, for example, we have seen the highest rate of police killings since 2001.

---

8.   FHC refers to former Brazilian president and academic Fernando Henrique Cardoso, who made significant contributions to dependency theory.

Do you believe that the argument for strengthening the State in order to return to the conditions prior to the collapse of the "progressive governments," has helped to produce the current situation? And what can you say about the experiences in autonomy with regard to self-defense and collective care, including in terms of security and self-defense to sustain life together in the face of the strengthening immunological, securitizing, surveillant, and racist culture?

A: I think that with the global crisis of 2008, the internal crisis of June 2013, and the fall of the PT, a cycle of post-dictatorship democracies has ended. The governability, hegemony, and a certain consensus that the State has relied upon is no longer there. Therefore, I do not find a pure form of domination that reflects a kind of prolonged crisis of governmentality, in the sense that Foucault described. What I find is that the State relies less on consensus as it does the necessary governing techniques capable of creating the conditions that make the system work.

For movements, the challenge is to detach from the old two-step strategy (as Wallerstein analyzes) to focus on other ways of doing politics, ways that do not exclude a relationship with the State and governments but are also not simply organized around that.[9] The question is: then what is the way? We must invent it, but not reinvent it or start from scratch, rather we should be basing these politics on what the pueblos have done and what they are currently doing and undertaking today.

Let's look at what is occurring under the pandemic in southern Colombia, in Cauca, among the Nasa, Misak, and Coconuco peoples, for which we turn to the Regional Indigenous Council of

---

9.   The two-step process of revolution: gain control of the State and then transform the world.

Cauca (CRIC). In fact, in the context of the 2019–2020 national protests, where hundreds of thousands of Colombians took to the streets to protest the government of President Iván Duque Márquez, at least four territories of the Cauca region decided to return to the criteria of "self-governance." They undertook an inward minga or collective practice within their community that consists of a process of collective harmonization within and across communities and nature. The Association of Ancestral Authorities Nasa Çxhâçxha, which promotes these governments, maintains that "the cabildo is not ours, it is something imposed from outside," so in June 2021 it carried out "a process of mingas of thought hand in hand with the elderly," to strengthen autonomy from the spiritual orientation of the most experienced community members.[10] Around stoves, they light incense of traditional healing plants and gather with medicine peoples near lagoons and sacred sites. Here, community is a healing and caring principle. They also intensify and diversify crops, send food to urban Indigenous people, and exchange it for sanitary products. They barter between producers working in different climate zones, without the use of money and in accordance with their needs. They closed the territory and mobilized seven thousand Indigenous Guard to control seventy points of entry and exit of the reservations. They see barter as an anti-neoliberal economic and political alternative. The topic of barter fairs are elaborated on in subsequent chapters.

In close relationship with the self-defense groups, autonomous movements have been multiplying. In the north of Peru, the Autonomous Territorial Government of the Wampis Nation

---

10. Comunicaciones Nasa Çxhâçxha, "PEBI-CRIC Realizó el III Encuentro Regional de Educación en el Marco de las Normas del SEIP," Nasa Çxhâçxha website, June 30, 2021, https://tierradentro.co/pebi -cric-realizo-el-iii-encuentro-regional-de-educacion-en-el-marco-de -las-normas-del-seip.

is one of the most recent examples, having been founded in 2018. In 2022, three other Amazonian peoples are on the same path. In addition to these, there are many more autonomous zones that are defining their autonomy in similar yet unique ways. These unique mobilizations warrant a different kind of understanding and interpretation. How do we define what is today happening between the Munduruku or the Tupi-Nambá of the Serra do Padeiro in Bahia? Or in a few quilombos in Brazil and in other places throughout the continent? As dispossession and the extreme right continue to advance, the pueblos intensify their autonomous turn, for the simple fact that they have no other way of defending themselves in order to survive as pueblos.

Q: Reflecting on the movements and revolts associated with Indigenous peoples is very important in your work. What is unique about the experience not only of Indigenous peoples, but of all pueblos who are more distinct from what we refer to as the West, and what in these experiences can lead to an expansion of ways of thinking and doing politics? What are the dialogues and desirable encounters between these forms of struggle and the traditions of left-wing movements of European origin in the face of the profound erosion of democratic structures that is currently taking place today in Latin America and across the world?

A: I believe the desired encounters necessarily involve territories, the territorialization of peoples, of all classes, colors, and genders. I would say that without territories we are nothing, and if we fail to anchor ourselves as collective subjects we vanish into thin air, as Marx said. The working class was defeated when its spaces, such as the taverns, were neutralized and when the factory was deterritorialized, fragmenting the production process. The workers' force was never just in the factory. Without the working-class neighborhood, without the dense sociability between families, there would never have been anything that we could call workers' power. The soviets were territorial, they corresponded to a working-class region, like the industrial belts in Allende's Chile or the ABC region of São Paulo during the dictatorship.[11]

There is a fantasy that speaks of the unions as key to the class struggle, something that real research on the working class does not demonstrate. The power of the class was found in their territorial communities, many of them around or near the factories. In fact, syndicalists continue to exist, but since there are no worker-centered communities, they do not have the slightest strength, not even representativeness. I spent seven years studying a working-class community in a small town, which revolved around two factories, the largest in their field in Uruguay.[12] I consulted thirty years' worth of trade union archives and came to see how the union was a shell that was dedicated to simply negotiating with the bosses, while the workers in the lowest rungs turned the factory upside down with wildcat strikes, standing off against the despotism of the foremen. People do not directly revolt against a system, at least not initially, but rather against concrete forms of oppression: that of the overseers, of the cops as is now being carried out in the US, of misogynist men, of the direct and oppressive power above them. There is no such thing as a struggle against patriarchy or against capitalism in the abstract, except in the minds of some left-wing intellectuals. One of the conclusions I came to understand is that the struggle was more powerful when the workers were a multitude (organized informally in their networks of "natural" friendships),

---

11. The ABC region refers to the greater region of São Paolo that is centered around Industrial development: Santo André, São Bernardo do Campo, and São Caetano do Sul.
12. Raúl Zibechi, *De Multitude a Clase: Formación y Crisis de una Comunidad Obrera, Juan Lacaze (1905–2005)* (Montevideo: Ediciones Ideas, 2006).

than when they became a hierarchical and institutionalized "class" under the union.

Today I find movements reviving their territoriality. Movements in Europe are increasingly territorial, especially after the 2008 crisis. You can see this with the rise in urban and peri-urban gardens, public spaces recovered by neighbors for noncommercial leisure, as well as self-managed buildings, factories, and recovered haciendas, and even an entire neighborhood in Vitoria, Errelakeor (neighborhood in the Basque country of Spain). I have seen this in Italy, Greece, and the Spanish State, places that had previously not had such initiatives.

With this territorialization, the link between movements in Europe and Latin America begins to change. Before, the relationship was based upon their solidarity with us, which is maintained but is typically unilateral and monetary, leading to very ugly situations in which some people take advantage, and many are left out. This is one of the things that led the Zapatistas to create the juntas de buen gobierno, to overcome the sacrosanct solidarity of the institutional left and NGOs. Now we begin to do other more interesting things: exchange experiences, learn how place-based pueblos are overcoming difficulties and building much deeper and more creative types of bonds.

Q: In your analysis of autonomous movements, you locate the centrality of territory, describing it with the metaphor of the coffer, a space for people to protect themselves from the capitalist flood. At the same time that this notion dialogues with the ongoing climate crisis, it opens space for a more radical reading of this current epoch. The Yanomami shaman and spokesperson Davi Kopenawa has been saying that the rampant increase in capitalist destruction means that there is no safe place to take refuge. Whether in cities or forests, the sky will fall on everyone's head. In this way, how can we begin to think about political actions produced by these sites of refuge that look beyond themselves? Actions that may have the potential to intervene in a world on the verge of having the sky fall upon it.

A: It is evident that the pueblos(the people) know much more than we do. What Davi says is completely true. An external material world no longer exists. Moreover, and this is significant, destruction no longer depends solely on capital but on what disturbed the Italian poet Pasolini: the anthropological mutation pushed through by consumerism. Trying to avoid ecological collapse is futile, because we would need to convince a majority of the world's population to take another course, an impossible task. The degradation of the human being is to such an extent that you would not be able to alter current lifeways without catastrophic consequences. Moreover, I doubt that a catastrophe can change us. In that sense, I disagree with thinkers like the philosopher Žižek, whose thoughts seem to me to lead to nothing because they are not grounded in reality. I am here referring to statements he has made about this current crisis leading people to rethink their ways. No, it doesn't work that way because the system has locked us up and left us a diabolical window: the internet.

It is the greatest drug ever invented. Those who are doing something different are, precisely, the peoples who have a "lack" of internet, those who do not depend on it because they have terrible or no connection or because they live in nature, which is far superior to the screen, because it connects our hearts and emotions with ourselves, our friends, our colleagues, and with the whole world. Our emotions invoked by the natural world, like the emotion of love, are irreplaceable and only when we amputate ourselves from that dimension do we become prisoners of something as poor as a screen.

For more than twenty-five years the Zapatistas have tried to do what you say, to join with others to make some sort of intervention onto the political scene. The result, as you know, has been very poor. Here I want to propose something different from what Davi says: it is true that there are no safe places anymore, but we can create them. If we do not, we stand to disappear as a species, at least as the community that we as human beings have been thus far until not so long ago. I want to say that the Wampis government, the territories of the Serra do Padeiro, the Nasa, and Zapatista autonomous communities in the last three decades are spaces and territories that have never previously existed.

As far as I can guess, I imagine only a few interventions in that direction would be able to create such kinds of safe spaces, not for technical reasons but politically, based upon bonds of trust and community. These coffers are not strong constructions with bomb or tsunami-proof materials, but links solid enough to resolve the problems between those of us who are in these territories of resistance.

Q: In conventional left movements in Latin America there is still a tendency that, despite various tactical and strategic differences, acts through political forms that seek to unify, homogenize, and reduce differences. In many social movements, images of "politicization" most often have to do with the process carried out by external centripetal forces that are set up to integrate "parts" into the "whole." They seek to make sense of the "disorganized" individuals who they find to be too connected to "experience" and "needs," aspects these movements believe must be overcome in order for this political dysfunctionality to become "majorities." In your texts, however, you draw attention to the existence of another way of thinking and doing politics and that does not go through this reverence for an ideal "One," as the anthropologist Pierre

Clastres would put it but for the power to be *an* other, to produce differences: "a world where many worlds fit," as the Zapatistas say. Thus, you document ways of doing politics that are not separated from everyday life. On the contrary, they are made through it, a politics that does not oppose the imperatives of struggle against the power of differentiation of life but makes this relationship its greatest strength.

Would it be possible to think of this as one of the most significant contrasts in the revolutionary imagination today? What would be the most outstanding successes of movements that are not allowing themselves to be hijacked by an ideal "One," by the need to be a State, and that could possibly expand the revolutionary imaginary of the left that is today so impoverished?

A: In addition to avoid falling into the concept of one State, party, or revolutionary army, I think we should avoid the idea of there being *one* society. Both ideas should go together. Rejecting unity and homogenization goes hand in hand and implies betting on diversity and a concept of totality that is different from the one we inherited from Europe. These are themes that I draw from the work of Peruvian sociologist Aníbal Quijano, who describes a totality composed of parts that are not identical but heterogeneous. Here the concept of heterogeneity is as important as that of totality.

A few examples for elaboration. In homogeneous societies, the whole is imposed on the parts because there is only one logic and thus it is that the parts have characteristics similar to the whole, to the point that the whole is in the parts, and these are parts of the whole. But in our Latin America, where we have an enormous historical heterogeneity (peoples who come from several continents with diverse histories), as well as structural heterogeneity (five labor relations, four of them not based on the wage), the totality is unable to reflect that diversity.[13] We see this with the plurinational states (of Bolivia and Ecuador for example) that remain composed of the state matrix, simply adorned with different colors. That is why, as Quijano says, revolution cannot consist in leaving behind one sort of totality (capitalism) from the social scenario to replace it with another kind of totality (socialism, for example). That doesn't work, nor can it work: "The processes of change cannot consist in the transformation of a historically homogeneous totality into an equivalent one, either gradually and continuously, or by leaps and ruptures," says Quijano.

This is what we see in [grassroot] feminisms and what I experienced in Chiapas. It is clear that the world of women changes, but in a very heterogeneous way. It is impossible for all women, of all ages, all social, geographical, and diverse peoples, to move in the same direction at the same time. Change would have to be imposed, as was done in the Soviet Union. Mapuche women have a history and workers another, and very different family relationships and social relations and with very different and even contradictory mediums.

In the Zapatista communities, heterogeneity predominates. It is very difficult to find a community in which all the families are Zapatistas. There the issue is how to build relationships with those who are pro-government or indifferent, or evangelical, or whatever the case may be. In addition, Mayan people in each geography face things in different ways, even if they are Zapatistas.

In short: we are still too Eurocentric, too committed to an ideal *one* or whole, thinking that it is still possible to speak in Latin America of a society in which we all feel a part of. That this still happens after five centuries may be demoralizing, but the reality is undeniable.

---

13. These are the five forms of control and exploitation of labor: wages, slavery, servitude, reciprocity, and petty commodity production, the last of which is commonly referred to as informality.

Only the Pueblos can Properly Defend Life and Territory

In many regions of Latin America, national states do not protect their citizens, particularly those in what are referred to as the popular sectors (*sectores populares*), Indigenous and Black peoples and mestizos, who are unprotected against the violence of drug trafficking, criminal gangs, private guards of multinational companies, and, paradoxically, the armed institutions of the State such as the police and the armed forces.[14]

The multiple massacres that have occurred in Mexico, such as that of forty-three students in Ayotzinapa in September 2014, are no exception, and it is with impunity that more than thirty thousand have disappeared and two hundred thousand have died since the State declared the "war on drugs" in 2007.[15] With some local particularities, what happens in Mexico is repeated in most countries throughout the region. In Brazil, sixty thousand people die under state or other kinds of institutional and organized violence every year, 70 percent of those are Afro-descendants, with most of them being younger and from impoverished communities.[16]

Faced with the panorama of violence that puts the lives of the most vulnerable populations at risk, some of the affected sectors have decided to create forms of self-defense and counterpowers. At first, they were defensive formations, but as they developed, they were able to manage real kinds of powers that

14. This section was originally published as "People in Defence of Life and Territory: Counter-Power and Self-Defence in Latin America" as part of the Transnational Institute's online collection *State of Power 2018*, https://longreads.tni.org/stateofpower/people-defence-life-territory.

15. "Año 11 de la Guerra Contra el Narco," *El País*, December 3, 2016, https://elpais.com/especiales/2016/guerra-narcotrafico-mexico.

16. Daniel Cerqueira et.al., *Atlas da Violência 2017* (Rio de Janeiro: Instituto de Pesquisa Econômica Aplicada and Fórum Brasileiro de Segurança Pública, 2017), http://www.ipea.gov.br/portal/images/170609_atlas_da_violencia_2017.pdf.

were established parallel to the State. The self-defense groups were necessary formations created in order to confront the hegemonic powers that were centered on state institutions. They challenge this hegemony with power anchored in community practices. However, in order to unravel what this new trend of societies in movement in Latin America is all about, we must analyze them on a deeper level.[17]

State logic and community logic are opposites, antagonistic in many cases. The first rests on the monopoly of legitimate force in a given territory and on its administration through a permanent, nonelectable civil and military bureaucracy that reproduces and is controlled by itself. The bureaucracy grants stability to the State, since it remains unchanged despite changes in government. Transforming it from within is very difficult and involves long-term processes. In Latin America, another factor is added that makes it even more difficult to change them: state bureaucracies are colonial creations, whose personnel are confined among white, educated, and male elites in countries where the population is mostly Black, Indigenous, and mestizo.

Community logic is based on the rotation of tasks and functions among all the members of a community, whose highest authority is the assembly. In this sense, the assembly as space/ time for decision making, should be considered a "common good." However, I do not consider the community solely as an institution but as a set of social relations that unfold in a given space or territory.

In a view focused on linkages, we cannot reduce the commonality to collectively owned areas, buildings, and elected authorities in assemblies that can be managed by caudillos or bureaucrats. We

---

17. In the original text I spoke of "social movements," a concept that I began to replace with "societies in movement" after an exchange with students from the Micaela Bastidas University in Apurímac, Peru.

can consider that a community can exist as two main types, as an institution and as a social bond, and that their difference is very important for the question of power. In the analysis I propose that the heart of the community is not in the commonly held property (although that property will continue to be important) but in the collectivity or the elements of and the work in community. Moreso, in trying to understand these practices, it is important that they not be reduced to institutionalized forms of cooperation as such work is known in traditional communities.[18]

Collective practices (*trabajo colectivo*) are the sustenance of the common and the true material basis that produces and reproduces the existence of living communities, with relations of reciprocity and mutual help that stand in contrast to the hierarchical and individuated and proper relations in state institutions. The community is kept alive not by common property but by collective works that are a creating, recreating, and affirming it in their daily lives. These collective works are how the common folks make community, as a way of expressing social relations different from the hegemonic ones.

In her sociological work, Guatemalan Mayan community member Gladys Tzul Tzul asserts that in the society based on communal work there is no separation between the sphere of domestic society, which organizes reproduction, and political society, which organizes public life but that both sustain and feed each other. In the communities, the complementarity between the two groups managed through communal governing, in what is known as the K'iche concept of *K'ax K'ol* discussed earlier, loosely translating to laborious work.[19]

---

18. Raúl Zibechi, "Los Trabajos Colectivos Como Bienes Comunes Material/Simbólicos," *El Apantle* 1 (October 2015).

19. Gladys Tzul Tzul, "Sistemas de Gobierno Comunal Indígena: La Organización de La Reproducción de La Vida," *El Apantle* 1 (October 2015).

Collective works are found in all the actions of the community, but there are those that make space not only for the reproduction of material goods but the community as such, from the assembly and the celebration to the consolation during periods of mourning and burials. There are also the types of collective labor that coordinate alliances with other communities. Additionally, many of the ongoing struggles of resistance ensuring the reproduction of communal life are also anchored in collective work.

Understanding community through the multiplicity of collective practices allows us to approach the question of power and counterpower from different places other than its general conceptualizations under critical thought. Most importantly, we find that neither power nor counterpower are here understood as institutions but as social relations. Second, being social relations, they can be produced by any collective subject in any given space as these kinds of relations are unfixed or not committed to place, from property relations and its authorities to reappearing wherever the subjects or movements carry out these types of practices inspired by their communal nature, even if they are not communities.

Third, by focusing on social relations we can approach flows of power, changes in power relations, and, in the case of social movements, the cycles of birth, maturity, and decline that are inherent in collective social logic. In this way, we will not be deceived by institutions that are actually linked to the state machinery as happens, for example, with the communal councils in Venezuela. In this case, the communal councils depend on state financing and function in a bureaucratic way. These councils form part of the organizational structure of the State, which strengthens the State but does not transcend it, registering a growing homogenization and loss of independence with time. Although in Venezuela there is a strong egalitarian culture in popular neighborhoods, where horizontality and the absence of hierarchies are the culture, councils are ultimately organizing under a belief that the contradictions between base and vertex have been resolved with the new path that egalitarian spaces have now constrained and controlled.[20]

A serious problem for emancipation in Latin America is that in all cultures there are more or less powerful variants of hierarchical culture, nourished by patriarchal and macho relations at all levels. Even in Indigenous communities and in spaces of Afro-descendants, where *caudillismo*, personality cults, and paternalism are reproduced and naturalized. That is why I think it is important to emphasize the social bonds that are expressed in "collective work," in its broadest sense, from assembly to party formations. It is in living and creative work that there is some possibility of modifying cultures and ways of doing, not in established institutions that function on the basis of inertia reproducing oppressions.

To avoid confusion, I will refer to the collective practices that both rural and urban communities are adopting as nonstate powers, taken up to defend themselves against superior powers that threaten their survival. In the examples that follow, there are a handful of spaces where anti-state power is deployed in such a way that they remain accountable to popular collectives (or communities).

It is important to note that in cities (such as Cherán and Mexico City), counterpowers are embedded in territorialized social movements that control common spaces and, therefore, stand to defend them. At this point, there are many similarities between what happens in rural Indigenous communities and in popular sectors of an urban periphery. The collective life of both is threatened by the same extractivist model (accumulation by dispossession) in two variants: hydroelectric dams and open-pit mining, in the rural case, and real estate speculation or gentrification, in the cities.

---

20.   Stefano Boni, *Il Poder Popular nel Venezuela Socialista del Ventunesino Secolo* (Florence: Editpress, 2017).

Self-defense and Social Movements

The Indigenous Guard of the Cauca region in Colombia are not an exception. There are many Latin American movements that have equipped themselves with forms of self-defense for the protection of their communities and their territories. The recent advance of extractivism, with its new mining ventures, monocultures, and infrastructure projects, is coming up against pueblos that, in some cases, have established forms of territorial control based on groups managed directly by the communities.

To better explain what these self-defense groups look like and how their social relations of power are generated, I will briefly describe four cases that complement the aforementioned one of the Indigenous Guard of southern Colombia: the peasant patrols (Rondas Campesinas) of Peru, the Community Police of Guerrero (Mexico), and two examples from urban peripheries, the bonfire guards in Cherán, Mexico, and the brigades of the Acapatzingo Housing Community in Mexico City.

Rondas Campesinas

During the 1970s, in remote rural areas of Peru where the State was seldom present, peasants found themselves unprotected against cattle rustlers. These remote areas were very poor and fragile communities, composed of cattle ranchers at high altitudes, and any kind of theft could disorganize their subsistence economy.

In these circumstances and seeking a practical solution to their vulnerability, assemblies decided to make night rounds, keeping watch for cattle rustlers and taking care of the communities' safety. The Rondas Campesinas were first installed as rotating night patrols among all the residents of the numerous communities, but then they began to carry out types of collective work to support the community (such as building roads and schools) and later began to serve as judicial forces by handing out communal punishment for banditry and other transgressions. In this way, the Rondas acted as a kind of local power.[21]

The Rondas were reactivated in Cajamarca in northern Peru, against the Conga gold mining project, to protect against the contamination of their water sources that family farming depended on. They decided to name themselves "Guardians of the Lagoons" because they camped up at four thousand meters in elevation, in inhospitable areas where very few people live, to watch, to witness, and resist the presence of multinationals.[22]

Community Police of Guerrero

The process of the Community Police of Guerrero, Mexico, deserves a similar reflection, although they do have quite distinctive characteristics from other self-defense organizations. The Regional Coordinator of Community Authorities-Community Police (Crac-PC) was born in 1995 in Indigenous communities to defend themselves against crime. It was initially made up of twenty-eight communities and managed to reduce crime rates by 90 to 95 percent.[23] At first, they handed over the criminals to the Public Ministry, but after seeing that they were released within hours, a regional assembly decided in 1998 to create the "Houses of Justice" where the accused could defend himself in his own language. In these houses of justice, the accused did not need to pay lawyers or fines, since community justice here meant the

---

21. Raphael Hötmer, "Las Rondas Campesinas No Son Grupos Terroristas," *Contrapunto* 4 (May 2014).
22. David Verstockt, "Los Guardianes de Las Lagunas—Conga—31-10-2012," video, October 31, 2012, https://www.youtube.com/watch?v=spqhNSMFT7M.
23. La Comisión para el Desarrollo de los Pueblos Indígenas, "Policia Comunitaria de Guerrero: Comprometida con el Pueblo, Parte 1," video, February 7, 2013, https://www.youtube.com/watch?v=cJmoXiJo6lk.

"re-education" of the convicted. Conviction did not mean punishments, rather they sought to reach agreements and conciliate the parties involved, bringing relatives and authorities of the communities into the process.

The "re-education" of the guilty consists of working in service for the community that was harmed, as communities saw justice beyond its punitive character, understanding its central purpose as the transformation of the individual under the supervision and monitoring of the communities. The highest authority of the Crac-PC is the open assembly that is organized in localities that have the community police. The assemblies "appoint coordinators and commanders, and have the power to dismiss them if they are accused of failing to do their duty; In addition, decisions are made related to the delivery of justice in difficult and sensitive cases, or to important matters of concern to the organization."[24] The Crac-PC has never generated a vertical and centralized command structure, a key difference in their function's power than that of the State.

Since 2011, the community police has served as a model that has expanded significantly across the state of Guerrero and throughout the country, as state violence and drug trafficking deepened along with the delegitimization of state apparatuses. In 2013 there was a huge leap in the number of self-defense groups (of which community police are included) in the state of Guerrero, with forty-six of the eighty-one municipalities having community police organizations involving some twenty-thousand armed citizens.

It is important to note that not all self-defense groups found in Latin America are organized as community police, as the latter is

---

24. Daniele Fini, "Policía Comunitaria de Guerrero: Una Institución de los Pueblos para la Seguridad y Justicia Desde Abajo," *Regeneración*, November 29, 2016, https://www.regeneracionlibertaria.org/policia -comunitaria-de-guerrero-una-institucion-de-los-pueblos-para-la -seguridad-y-justicia-desde-abajo.

mainly distinguished by their systematized training and use of weapons. Self-defense groups are groups of citizens who carry symbolic weapons and communications tools to defend themselves against the encroachment of the State and private or paramilitary forces, but unlike community police, their members are not appointed by their peoples or accountable to them as they are constantly rotating. However, their notable expansion is due to the growth of the Indigenous self-defense groups promoted by the Zapatista uprising of 1994 and recognized by the Ostula Manifesto of 2009, which was later approved by communities and Indigenous peoples from nine states at the twenty-fifth assembly of the National Indigenous Congress (CNI), which decreed the right to self-defense.[25]

Cherán's Bonfires

Cherán is a small city of fifteen thousand inhabitants in the state of Michoacán, Mexico, whose population are mostly of the Purépecha native community. On April 15, 2011, the population rose up against loggers who had long been terrorizing their community. Hundreds organized in defense of their forests that were used in common. For them, this was a stand in defense of life and communal security and against an organized crime that was protected by political power. Since that uprising, the community governs itself, and political and administrative discussions are held around the 179 bonfires that have been installed in four neighborhoods throughout the city, serving as the nucleus of Indigenous nonstate power.[26]

They hold elections to select a "Major Council" through a system of *usos y costumbres*, which is the highest municipal authority

---

25. National Indigenous Congress, "Manifesto of Ostula," Enlace Zapatista (blog), June 17 2009, http://enlacezapatista.ezln.org.mx/2009/06/17/manifiesto-de-ostula.

26. VICE en Español, "Cherán: El Pueblo Purépecha En Rebeldía," video, May 6, 2016, https://www.youtube.com/watch?v=Dql9_kKBwws.

that is recognized in the region, even by state institutions. Elections with traditional political parties are no longer held but they convene assemblies that elect the rulers. The bonfires, an extension of the communal kitchens set up in community barricades, became a space for coexistence between neighbors, a place for exchange and discussion, where "children, young people, women, men, and the elderly are actively included" in decision making.[27]

The image of communal power in Cherán is a set of concentric circles. At the core is the Municipal Assembly, supported by the Major Council of the Communal Government composed of twelve representatives, three from each neighborhood. Then the Operating Council and the Communal Treasury follow, forming the first circle around the center/assembly. Around it there are six more councils: Administrative council; the council of the Commons; the council of Social, Economic, and Cultural programs; the Justice council; the council of Civil Affairs; and the Neighborhood Coordinating Council. Finally, this is all separate among the four neighborhoods that constitute the outer circles, with the Municipal Assembly at its core. As they say in Cherán, it is a circular, horizontal, and articulated government structure.[28]

Acapatzingo

The Acapatzingo Housing Community is made up of six hundred families and is located in the southern area of Mexico City (which has twenty-three million inhabitants). This housing community belongs to the Francisco Villa Popular Organization of

27. Agencia SubVersiones, Cooperativa Cráter Invertido, and TV Cherán, "Cheran K'eri: Cuatro Años Construyendo Autonomía," SubVersiones, April 21, 2016, https://subversiones.org/archivos/115140.
28. Concejo Mayor de Gobierno Comunalde Cherán, *Cherán K'eri. 5 Años de Autonomía* (Cherán, Michoacán: Concejo Mayor de Gobierno Comunalde Cherán, 2017), https://www.academia.edu/40236872/Cher%C3%A1n_Keri_5_a%C3%B1os_de_autonom%C3%ADa.

the Independent Left (Organización Popular Francisco Villa de la Izquierda Independiente) and is the most consolidated popular neighborhood of urban Mexico, rooted in autonomy and self-organization. Its bases are the brigades formed by twenty-five families in the region. Each brigade appoints heads for the four general commissions: press, culture, surveillance, and maintenance. Their members rotate and appoint representatives to the general counsel of the entire settlement where representatives of all the brigades converge.

When a conflict arises, the brigade intervenes, even if it is an intrafamily problem. Depending on the seriousness of the conflict, the intervention of the supervisory commission and even the general council may be requested. Once a month a different brigade is selected for the responsibility of the security of people's property, but the concept of surveillance is not the traditional one of control, since this concept of surveillance revolves around the self-protection of the community, and its main work consists of carrying out political education.[29]

The supervisory commission holds the responsibility of marking and delineating the inside and the outside of the community, keeping track of those who can enter and those who should not. This is a central aspect of autonomy, perhaps the most important. The supervisory commission has implemented various accountability protocols including some that involve the younger members of the families. When an instance of domestic violence or aggression occurs, the children go out into the street and blow a whistle, a mechanism that the community uses in cases of emergencies. The interior environment is remarkably peaceful, it is quite common to see children playing alone with total tranquility in a safe space

29. César Enrique Pineda, "Acapatzingo: Construyendo Comunidad Urbana," *Contrapunto* 3 (November 2013).

protected by the community, something unthinkable in violent Mexico City.

❀ ❀ ❀

Since the 2008 financial crisis, some movements in the global North have taken very similar initiatives to those of Latin America's pueblos. The most notable feature is the territorialization of some resistances and collective projects, seen for example in places like Greece, Italy, and the Spanish State. This type of temporal organization brings resonance between the movements of the South and the North, not because they are identical but because they face similar problems and address them in quite similar ways.

The Azienda Mondeggi, a bankrupt and abandoned farm near Florence, Italy, has been reclaimed by dozens of young people, who produce wine, olive oil, and honey, among other products. They live collectively and have managed to reclaim dozens of hectares, turning them into "common goods."[30] Another remarkable collective territorial experience is the Non-TAV movement that is resisting high-speed rail in northern Italy, in the Susa Valley.[31] In Vitoria, Spain, young people from popular movements have recovered an entire neighborhood (Errekaleor) where they are defending themselves from real estate speculation.[32]

In these three European countries there are recovered factories, as well as hundreds of social and cultural centers in operation. In

30. Riccardo Botazzo, "La fattoria senza padroni," *Frontiere*, October 16, 2016, http://frontierenews.it/2016/10/ chianti-mondeggi-fattoria-senza -padroni.

31. Livio Pepino and Marco Revelli, *Non Solo un Treno: La Democrazia alla Prova della Val Susa* (Torino: Edizioni Gruppo Abele, 2012).

32. Raúl Zibechi, "Dos Continentes, una Misma Lucha," *Desinformémonos*, May 2, 2016, https://desinformemonos.org/dos-continentes-una-misma -lucha.

some Spanish cities, including Salamanca and Valencia, the unemployed work in semi-urban gardens to ensure food and minimum income. Some of these experiences are of a collective nature, linked to broader social movements.[33] As the cities of the North are being reshaped by real estate speculation, young people and women who only have access to low-quality jobs tend to open spaces of various kinds from gardens to cultural and alternative communication collectives, as a way of maintaining social relations of camaraderie and solidarity.

Power/Counterpower and Nonstate Powers

In this section I elaborate on my earlier introduction to nonstate powers, particularly contrasting this term with conventional forms of power. In a very general sense, we can argue that social movements are counterpowers that seek to balance or counterbalance the great global powers (multinational companies) and the powers of the State that usually work together. Often these counterpowers are quite symmetrical to state power, establishing very similar hierarchies even if they are occupied by people from excluded sectors of society, including other ethnicities, genders, and generations than those in power. Put simply, the concept of counterpower refers to a power that seeks to displace the existing power and is constituted in a very similar way to state power as we know it and suffer by it, at least in Western societies.[34]

---

33. Fernando Bellón, "Los Yayo-Okupas de Huertos Urbanos en Valencia," *Agroicultura-Perinquiets*, http://agroicultura.com/general/los-yayo-okupas-de-huertos-urbanos-en-valencia.

34. This is not to take up a theoretical debate about power, counterpower, or anti-power, theses defended by Antonio Negri and John Holloway respectively. Antonio Negri, "Contrapoder," in *ContraPoder: Una Introdución* (Buenos Aires: Ediciones de Mano en Mano, 2001) and

I think the big problem with these main conceptualizations of power that emanate from the predominant sociological and political traditions of the North is that they ignore the Latin American reality, where social movements are not constituted by collections of individuals but by families. When you go to an Indigenous community, to a camp of landless peasants, homeless, or unemployed, they always tell you "We are [so many] families." Families make up a community—not as an essentialist institutional community but as a community made up of strong and direct, face-to-face relationships between people who exercise close relationships in everyday life.

In the proposals of left groups and organizations that bet on "counterpower," there exists the tendency to become a new power, often built in the image and likeness of the nation-state they are opposing. The historical example would be the soviets of Russia or the Committees for the Defense of the Revolution (CDR) in Cuba, which over time became part of the state apparatus, subordinating themselves to the State and becoming part of its institutionality.

Communities in resistance in many places across Latin America organize from concrete experiences, constructing their powers (whether their structures are forms of self-defense or social relations) on a completely different basis than other great revolutions or social movements. In the hegemonic political culture, the image of the pyramid that inspires the State and the Catholic Church is constantly replicated in the parties and in the unions, with astonishing regularity. The control of power goes through the highest point of that pyramid and all political action puts collective energies in that direction.

There are, however, other very different traditions, in which all the energy of the community is focused on preventing leaders

John Holloway, "Twelve Theses on Changing the World Without Taking Power," *The Commoner* 4 (May 2002), https://thecommoner.org/wp-content/uploads/2019/11/Twelve-Theses-Holloway.pdf.

from acquiring power as conventionally understood, that is, from approaching a state-type power, as the French anthropologist Pierre Clastres points out.[35] The community understands *itself* as a power, which includes various relations of power that gives them a different character than that of the State. Councils of elders elected, and rotating positions, form transparent powers that are permanently controlled by the community so that they retain accountability. Different relations of power are established so that these councils and other positions do not separate to exercise a power over the community, which is what characterizes the State with its unelected bureaucracies, separated from society and placed over the people.

In naming these types of powers we must differentiate them from the other ways of exercising power typically carried out by the State—this power otherwise is what I refer to as nonstate powers. Perhaps the best-known case is the good governance boards of the five Zapatista regions operating in its five caracoles.[36] The boards are integrated, with half of them composed of men and the other half women. They are elected from among the hundreds of members of the autonomous municipalities. The entire government team, twenty-four people in caracoles, changes once every eight days.

This system of rotation, as the Zapatista support bases like to refer to them, allows everyone to learn to govern after a certain time. The rotation is registered at the three levels of Zapatista self-government: in each community among the people who integrate it, in each autonomous municipality by the elected—revocable and rotating delegates—and in each region with the good

35. Raúl Zibechi, *Dispersing Power: Social Movements as Anti-State Forces* (Oakland: AK Press, 2010), 66.
36. Caracoles, or conch shells, are the name for the Zapatista communities, in part due to the way they are spatially constructed, which informs their way of being.

government board. There are more than a thousand communities, twenty-nine autonomous municipalities, and some three hundred thousand people who are governed in this way.

Two issues are worth noting here. The first is that it is the only case in all of Latin America where autonomy and self-government are expressed at three levels with the same assembly and rotating logic as in the local community. Of the 570 municipalities in the state of Oaxaca, 417 are governed by an internal regulatory system, known as usos y costumbres, which allows them to elect their authorities in a traditional way, in assembly and without political parties. But even in this widespread case of self-government, it was not possible to scale up and go beyond the municipal level.

The second characteristic of Zapatista autonomy is that it does not produce bureaucracies, because rotation disperses them, preventing a specialized and separate body from forming. Something similar happens in Cherán, between the Indigenous Guard of Colombia and the Guardians of the Lagoons in the Peruvian Andes. However, in the case of Colombia, there are no assemblies that govern a territory or reservation, which would be something similar to the Zapatista regions. However, the interference of the State through education and health plans, and especially through state funding of the councils, has led them to become bureaucratized although there are important counterprojects such as the Indigenous Guard, which is the heart of power of the Nasa ethnic group in the region.

The importance of nonstate powers, among which I include the various forms of self-defense organizations, lies in the fact that Latin American social movements currently have a twofold and complex dynamic. On the one hand, they interact with the State and its institutions, as every movement in history has done. It is a complex and changing relationship, varying by country and political realities. Nonstate powers resist the State and big business, they make proposals as well as demands, negotiate, and often obtain resources and approvals of the demands they have made out of their own platforms. This is most often seen in the trade union movement but is seen in the vast majority of movements as well.

The other part of the dynamic is more contemporary and has gained prominence in recent decades, especially in Latin America. Along with their fluid link to the State, the movements create their own spaces and territories, either by recovering lands that had been expropriated from them or by occupying idle land from private owners or official institutions in the most diverse rural and urban areas. About 70 percent of area of Latin American cities have been "takeovers" in which rural migrants build their unincorporated homes, their neighborhoods, and social infrastructure such as schools, health centers, and sports fields.

Many of these illegally occupied spaces are legalized by institutions that also offer collective services, but many others are repressed. Some of these spaces are formed with a different intention: they seek to create other forms of life, or "other worlds," in Zapatista language. They become "territories in resistance" that, in some cases, move toward "territories of emancipation," where women and young people play a prominent role in shaping the new society/territory.

What is evident is that the system pushes millions of people to create their own spaces and territories in order to survive because they have no housing, are unemployed, or suffer from other forms of marginalization. In these spaces they seek to build the health and education that the system denies them, either because it is of poor quality or because the services are very distant and difficult to access. In the five thousand rural settlements set up in Brazil by the Landless Peasant Movement (MST), for example, there are fifteen hundred schools with teachers born in the communities and trained in state teachers' colleges.

All of these constructions need to be defended. We are not dealing with exceptional situations. For seven months, between September 2017 and April 2018, thirty thousand people (eight thousand families) camped in an urban area of the city of São Bernardo do Campo, in São Paulo, Brazil, in what was known as the occupation of Pueblo Sin Miedo organized by the MTST (Homeless Workers Movement).[37] While they focus their energies on acquiring everyday necessities such as water, food, and hygiene, they were forced to defend their space from direct violence (several neighbors fired guns at the occupants). In order to deal with these existential threats, they established internal regulations to ensure safety and teamwork, and to create ways to make decisions and solve quotidian problems.[38] This led them to create a system of internal coordination, to elect their members and to support them for months at a time, what can be considered as an embryo of nonstate power. The paths are not predetermined, each concrete experience we find takes whatever paths it can or is defined by its members.

37. "Drone Filma Ocupação Gigante Em São Bernardo Do Campo," video, September 26, 2017, https://www.youtube.com/watch?v=3qBuPcOm KU4.

38. Taís Di Crisci, "Um grito por Dignidade: Conheça a Ocupação Povo sem Medo—São Bernardo do Campo," MTST website, October 4, 2017, https://mtst.org/mtst/um-grito-por-dignidade-conheca-a-ocupacao -povo-sem-medo-sao-bernardo-do-campo.

Rethinking Transition with Societies in Movement

Inertia is one of the great artisans of history.

—FERNAND BRAUDEL

The history of the workers' and socialist movements around the globe have been centered on an extensive debate about what the transition from a capitalist to socialist/post-capitalist society would look like and has focused mainly on theory bequeathed by Marx and Lenin.[1] The very concept of transition, elaborated by Marx, was widely debated by the main currents of the left of the twentieth century in light of some of the difficulties that arose during the Russian Revolution.

However, the debates were seemingly focused on the question of ownership of the means of production and exchange and on the "political economy of the transitional period," if such a thing can even be identified. My main issue of concern with the debates that occupied critical thinking since the Russian Revolution, and even before then, is the problem of "totality": the consideration that a given social formation can change as a whole toward a totally different social formation.

---

1. An earlier version of this essay was published in Spanish in *La Tizza Cuba*, on November 10, 2020, https://medium.com/la-tiza/repensando
    -la-transici%C3%B3n-con-los-pueblos-en-movimiento-a916f9e43eee.

Before entering into this debate, it seems necessary to me to highlight three aspects that the founders of socialism were not in a position to evaluate:

a) Eurocentrism is the most prominent, since they could not (or would not, in the case of Marx) establish a theory to be applied across all temporalities and places. This much is often left behind by many socialists ever since.

b) the nation-state as it actually existed in Latin America: because of its colonial makeup, the founders of socialism failed to see how the region's independence was "a rearticulation of the coloniality of power placed on to new institutional bases."[2]

c) historical experience: both the failure of Soviet and Chinese socialism, the emergence of Indigenous and Black peoples in Latin America, and also feminist movements that I believe have come to modify our conception of social conflict and the transition to a new world.

The first two aspects are well-known themes within the work of Peruvian sociologist Aníbal Quijano, and these themes find themselves in dialogue with the third. Expanding on my earlier introduction of his work, I was to bring forth Quijano's understanding of the totality from Latin America, which for him implies recovering the concept of the "structural historical heterogeneity" of our social formations. This heterogeneity could be summarized in the existence of five forms of control and exploitation of labor: wages, slavery, servitude, reciprocity, and small commodity production that we often refer to as "informality."

---

2.   Aníbal Quijano, "Colonialidad del poder, eurocentrismo y América Latina," in *Cuestiones y Horizontes: De la Dependencia Histórico-Estructural a la Colonialidad/Descolonialidad del Poder* (Buenos Aires: CLASCO, 2014).

It is important to remember that wage labor is not hegemonic but, above all, "it is not the only antagonistic or alternative form under capitalism."[3] However, critical theory has not reflected on, say, the role of reciprocity or small commodity production through subjects and in the transition to a new world. A whole tradition of the Latin American left mentions these social relations only as "pre-capitalist remnants," viewing them as a hinderance to the development of the productive forces. One of the greatest exponents of the communist current considered that, among the Latin American Indigenous population, "the institutions and social relations transplanted from late Spanish feudalism" predominate.[4] According to Rodney Arismendi, these residual political formations had to be swept away by the development of capitalism and could in no way be the basis for the construction of a new society.

Over the last fifty years in Latin America, diversities have emerged articulating heterogeneous sectors that cannot be reduced to parts of a whole since, as Quijano points out, each of them has a "relative autonomy" or, as he alternatively states, "it is a total unit in its own configuration, because it also has a historically heterogeneous constitution."[5] This can be observed with the deployment of Landless Peasant Movements (MST in Brazil, as an example), various movements led by Indigenous and Black communities, and increasingly in some urban peripheries throughout the continent. The Latin American totality supposes the articulation of heterogeneities that present logics or degrees of autonomy with respect to the whole, which in no way obey a homogeneous behavior. A reflection on the economies of the original peoples, the usos y

---

3.   Aníbal Quijano, "El Trabajo al Final del Siglo XX," in *Cuestiones y Horizontes: De la Dependencia Histórico-Estructural a la Colonialidad/Descolonialidad del Poder* (Buenos Aires: CLASCO, 2014), 274.

4.   Rodney Arismendi, *Lenin, La Revolución y América Latina* (Mexico City: Editorial Grijalbo: 1976), 286.

5.   Arismendi, *Lenin*, 355.

costumbres or the form of election of authorities, and their character, demonstrated the vast difference between Quijano's notion of totality against the European concept of totality.

Consequently, there can be no homogeneous transition, neither unilinear nor unidirectional nor one-dimensional, as Quijano mentions because we are facing movements that have diverse and even opposite logics. In short: change cannot imply "the complete exit from the historical scenario of a totality with all its components, so that another derivative of it takes its place."[6] To describe what real classes and social relations are like on our continent, he uses the terms "heterogeneous," "discontinuous," and "conflictive." Concepts that also apply to social change.

If we look at the reality of our continent, we will find that millions of people—landless peasants living in agrarian reform settlements in Brazil, Indigenous people living in communities in resistance, and Afro-descendant communities socializing in palenques and quilombos—are maintaining social relations that are quite different from the hegemonic ones, always already in conflict and dispute with capital and States. These families, these social sectors, or otherwise societies in movement, no longer live integrally within capitalism but in some hybrid form that cannot be determined theoretically except in concrete reference to the type of society—yes, society—that they are building.

These heterogeneities are not inherited or frozen realities, but processes in permanent construction-reconstruction due to social conflict: the Mapuche in Wallmapu (Chile) and the Nasa people in Colombia recover land almost permanently, as do the peasants, who must defend them and sometimes lose them. In a sea of rapacious racial and capital violence brought on by the State, these societies in movement construct islets and archipelagos of territories of

---

6.   Arismendi, *Lenin*, 355.

emancipation and resistance, spaces where use-values predominate over exchange values. They have at least two elements in common: the collective subjects have recovered land and other means of production, and in them the decisions are made by organized groups and collectives. This is their form of "power," or however they describe it, which is their way of collectively deciding and enforcing their decisions in delimited territories within the greater territory controlled by the nation-state.

An additional clarification. Power and State are not synonymous. Of course, the State is a form of power, anchored in the monopoly of legitimate violence in a given territory, exercised by a double civil and military bureaucracy, permanent and not elected or revocable. The peoples re-create nonstate powers, such as the communities and the Indigenous councils of Cauca that are equipped with Indigenous Guard; the Zapatista juntas of good government; the assemblies of peasant movements that, in Peru, for example, have their "peasant patrols" for the defense of their lands.[7]

In the following pages, I intend to enter the debate about the transition from capitalism to something beyond capitalism by anchoring myself in the concrete emancipatory practices of some peoples who have set themselves in motion. If you prefer, those practices are the epistemological place I choose to enter this debate.

Why do I take this path? I do not want to enter into theoretical debates that tend to lead to abstract philosophical convictions when I believe that the central thing is the concrete practice of millions of workers. It is a methodological bet that does not relegate the theoretical debate, but that subordinates it to the emancipatory tendencies of the antisystemic movements. What I propose, in a

---

7. Raúl Zibechi, "People in Defence of Life and Territory: Counter-Power and Self-Defence in Latin America," in *State of Power 2018*, Transnational Institute, https://longreads.tni.org/stateofpower/people -defence-life-territory.

way, is to draw a dialogue between the concrete practice of some movements and the debates on transition.

In Zapatista (EZLN) Territory

The community, 8 de Marzo (8th of May) of the autonomous municipality 17 de Noviembre (17th of November), is an hour by dirt roads from the Morelia caracol. Every family in this community has a plot of about five hectares with beans, corn, bananas, vegetables, fruits, and chickens. They also have a coffee plot in the mountains where they harvest to sell what they do not consume.

The community sits on what was the hacienda of Pepe Castellanos, brother of Absalon Castellanos, lieutenant colonel and a former governor of Chiapas. He was the owner of fourteen farms on land that was usurped by Indigenous families. His kidnapping by the Zapatistas in January 1994 led to landowners fleeing their large farming estates that were situated on the support bases of the Zapatistas.

The community has more than a thousand hectares of good land and they no longer have to work on the stony and arid slopes as they grow traditional foods. On the recommendation of the EZLN, they are now growing vegetables and fruits. They eat better and work collectively with much greater freedom than when they worked on the farm. The family that hosted me harvested six sacks of coffee, about three hundred kilos, of which they hold a sack for family consumption and sell the rest. Depending on the price, they manage to buy two or three cows with each harvest. "The cows are the bank and when we need anything we sell them," explain the villagers.[8]

---

8. Raúl Zibechi, "El Arte de Construir un Mundo Nuevo: La libertad

On the communal lands, they collectively work to harvest coffee which they sell and use the funds to buy horses and cows that then belong to the community. Among the families and community members they have about 150 horses and almost two hundred cattle. The women's group also has a coffee plantation as well as a community chicken coop. In this way, they have their own funds to attend workshops and women's meetings. In the community there are several trucks owned by families who were able to repair them and make them available to the collective. With surpluses and with contributions from international solidarity, they have managed to supply the clinics, which today have basic surgery, dental, gynecology, and ophthalmology services, as well as laboratories, herbal workshops, ambulances, ultrasound equipment, and patient beds.[9] Additionally, many families cover the expenses for transportation and accommodation for the broader population, fulfilling the duties of the three levels of self-government: the local or community, the autonomous municipalities, and the good government boards at the regional level.

The few products that families are unable to produce (salt, sugar, oil, and soap) are bought in the municipal capitals in "Zapatista stores" that are installed in zones that they occupied following the uprising in 1994. They have no need for external markets and preserve their economy within a circuit that they control, providing a self-sufficiency that though there is a market-based facet, there is no dependency.

---

según los Zapatistas," Centre Tricontinental, May 2, 2023, https://www.cetri.be/El-arte-de-construir-un-mundo.

9.   Orsetta Bellani, "Así se Cuidan del Covid-19 en Territorio Zapatista," *Pie de Página*, July 4, 2020, https://piedepagina.mx/asi-se-cuidan-del-covid-19-en-territorio-zapatista; Anya Briy, "Zapatistas: Lessons in Community Self-Organisation in Mexico," *Open Democracy*, June 25, 2020, https://www.opendemocracy.net/en/democraciaabierta/zapatistas-lecciones-de-auto-organización-comunitaria-en.

The stores are managed on a rotating basis by *comuneros*. The bases of support tell me that from time to time they have to work a month at the store of Al-tamirano, about an hour from their community. In that case, the community prolongs the *milpa* (crop harvesting system) for fifteen days to allow the *comuneros* to work at the stores or do other tasks. When someone is elected to a position on the good government board at Caracol Morelia for example, their chores are covered in the same way, which we can describe as a model of reciprocity.

Each community, no matter how small, has a school and a health clinic. In the 8 de Marzo community there are forty-eight families, not all of them Zapatistas. The assembly elects its authorities, half of whom are women and the other half men, as well as its teachers and those in charge of health care. No one can refuse to serve because it is seen as a service to the community and is vital to its integrity.

In the clinic, medicines from the pharmaceutical industry co-exist with a wide variety of medicinal plants. A very young girl is in charge of making syrups and ointments from local medicinal plants and a young man is typically in charge of allopathic medicine. The ward has a *huesero* (bone doctor or shaman) and a midwife, who make up the standard health team in the Zapatista communities. In general, they attend relatively simple cases and when they are overwhelmed, they transfer the patient to the larger clinic at the caracol. When they cannot solve a case, they go to one of the Zapatista hospitals or, in extreme cases, to the ones offered by the State.

The health work of Zapatismo has three aspects: resisting the domination of state health practices by affirming one's own identity, bringing health to all communities, and fighting patriarchy. The three aspects can be summarized in the strengthening of autonomy as is central for these "communities in rebellion." For this there are members who rely on and promote traditional knowledge (herbal, bone, midwifery), which are put into practice in a complementary way with allopathic medicine. Health sovereignty and autonomy is the answer to the humiliation and mistreatment that Indigenous peoples, and especially Indigenous women, have long suffered in state hospitals. Health is women's space of power: "Health work has given Zapatista women the confidence and ability to confront and renegotiate gender, ethnic, and class relations in their families, communities, and region."[10] Women have their own collective projects to fund travel for training courses and other organizational tasks. Here community health is built on the culture and experience of communities themselves.

If we focus on production and reproduction, we will find that the key to this "economy" is the collective works that, in the opinion of the Zapatistas, constitutes the "the engine of autonomy." The Zapatista economy is not an autonomous sphere nor is it governed by laws, rather it is within the communities that are permanently threatened by the Mexican State where production is at the service of resistance to the militaristic national government.

If we are to approach the question of autonomy with the conceptual tools of political economies, those that are elaborated in another historical context to account for another reality, we would not understand what happens in the autonomous territories of Chiapas. The analysis must focus on what organizes the life of the Zapatista communities in this region, and that is resistance.

Indeed, when they refer to their "projects for reproduction," they take them up under the label of "economic resistance," which has three distinct levels or areas: community economy, municipal

10. Melissa Forbis, "Autonomía y un Puñado de Hierbas: La Disputa por las Identidades de Género y Étnicas por Medio del Sanar," in *Luchas "Muy Otras": Zapatismo y Autonomía en las Comunidades Indígenas de Chiapas*, eds. Bruno Baronnet, Mariana Mora Bayo, and Richard Stahler-Sholk (Chiapas: Universidad Autónoma Metropolitana, 2011), 372.

economy, and zone-level economy—that is, from families to the boards of good government (*buen gobierno*): "We prepare from bases of families, as villages, as regions, and municipalities in the area; to be able to support our family, to be able to buy everything necessary for each family, so that when we have to do a job our family also feels supported in the struggle."[11]

Survival is ordered in relation to collective resistance that is grounded in community and centered around the proposal of autonomy. In everyday life, resistance consists of strengthening the community and working together with other communities, municipalities, and regions, because there is a belief that those who have responsibilities must move/act in order to fulfill them: "The communities have strengthened their economy by creating collective work, especially in the field. This has helped a lot in the struggle, it helps us for when supporting comrades who go out to carry out their work."[12]

Zapatista autonomy is largely defined by the modes of organization and resistance in their community culture, in which collective production is central. This culture is also reflected in the ways that local, municipal, and regional authorities are elected. "Being an autonomous authority is a commitment to the people and it involves sacrificing time for work and rest, and is not a source of power, privileges, and wealth."[13] Communal assemblies elect authorities at all levels of administration. In the community, it is the assembly that elects. The good government board is elected by the Zone Assembly, which is composed of the authorities of all the municipalities that comprise it. Once the proposed list of names is

11. EZLN, *Cuaderno de Texto de Primer Grado del Curso de "La Libertad Según L@s Zapatistas: Gobierno Autónomo, I* (Chiapas: EZLN, 2013), 6.
12. EZLN, *Cuaderno de Texto de Primer Grado*, 80.
13. Paulina Fernández Christlieb, *Justicia Autónoma Zapatista: Zona Selva Tzeltal* (Mexico City: Estampa Artes Gráficas, 2014), 122.

made, they are taken to the community assemblies where the support bases choose the people for each municipality and zone.[14]

In her meticulous work, Paulina Fernández Christlieb documents regions where the autonomous communities can elect more than forty positions (agents, commissioners, education and health committees, collective works), with their respective substitutes, secretaries, and treasurers, including between four and eight police officers. The same criterion is used to elect authorities and positions in autonomous municipalities and in the boards of good governance. "The autonomous police are not armed, nor uniformed, nor are they professionals," their presence is discreet, and they provide a free service to the community that has elected them.[15]

The Zapatista authorities work collectively and do not make individual decisions; "the fulfillment of their functions is monitored and qualified by the peoples who elected them, through the mechanisms of community democracy in perpetuity."[16] There are no single-person positions as the relationship between the various positions is structured horizontally and nonhierarchically, and there is permanent coordination between the teams of the different levels of autonomous government. Sooner or later all the authorities return to their community as support bases. We are facing a government that is not a State, nor a mechanism of power that separates and is placed above society. If capitalism is power, as Öcalan points out, it is a power anchored in the hierarchy of the "strong and cunning man" who, through force, has been able to "usurp social values." This is the "group of robber bandits," which the Kurdish leader calls "the forty thieves."[17]

14. Fernández, *Justicia Autónoma Zapatista,* 144.
15. Fernández, *Justicia Autónoma Zapatista,* 158.
16. Fernández, *Justicia Autónoma Zapatista,* 178.
17. Abdullah Öcalan, *Manifesto for a Democratic Civilization,* Vol. II, *Capitalism: The Age of Unmasked Gods and Naked Kings* (Porsgrunn, Norway: New Compass Press, 2017), 86.

Autochthonous Economies: Barter Systems and the Sovereign Economy

Among the various economic practices I would like to highlight are the "barter fairs," a form of exchange of products and knowledge between different communities and regions. Barter is one of the practices of their *economia propia* (loosely translated to the sovereign economy). The Tejido Económico Ambiental defines the community economy as "autonomy for life," which means they maintain harmony with nature with the aim of "living in joy, enjoying harmony where the material and the spiritual, energy and the cosmos, the tulle (orchard) and sacred sites, natural ordering, and community mandates are combined." In this process, because it is a process, "the community participates with its actions in the territory, with the daily encounter of the ancestral and the permanent coexistence with Mother Earth and other beings."[18]

Communities argue that barter is an anti-neoliberal political alternative. A member of the Association of Cabildos Ukawe's' Nasa C'hab explains: "A barter is made between products from different climates. Meeting and exchange points are established in which necessity and not value prevails because it is not about exchanging equivalences but exchanging what is needed."[19]

Barter is an ancestral practice, but it is also a form of solidarity and reciprocity that allows for the strengthening of one's own economy. As can be seen, the rejection of money, the exchange between products and crops from cold climates and hot climates, not for

18. Asociación de Cabildos Indígenas del Norte del Cauca (ACIN), "Tejido Económico Ambiental," Çxhab Wala Kiwe website, December 19, 2016, https://nasaacin.org/tejidos-y-programas/tejido-economico-ambiental.
19. Raúl Zibechi, "Los Pueblos En Movimiento Frente a La Violencia Sistémica," in *Poderes, Privilegios, Resistencias y Alternativas: Lectura Crítica en Tiempos de Post-Pandemia,* ed. Carlos Pástor Pazmiño (Buenos Aires: CLASCO, 2022), 233.

equivalences (kilo for a kilo) but giving priority to needs, implies that they are promoting noncapitalist social relations. In the same way, families organize to send food to Indigenous people who have migrated to cities such as Cali, Bogotá, and Popayán. In the region of Inzá, Tierradentro, eight hundred families from eight municipalities were organized to send thirty-six tons of cassava, bananas, panela, and other products, a shipment that was repeated for several weeks, with the aim of enhancing solidarity and nonmarket practices. One of the promoters of this barter system pointed out: "We are rich because we produce food. But the most important thing is not the material, but the brotherhood that is built, the spirituality that is cultivated. Barter helps us break the dynamics of individualism and strengthens the community."[20]

The peoples of Cauca once again consider barter as a strategy of resistance to the capitalist system as they did for a long time, although it has tended to weaken. I would like to emphasize that practices are changing, that social relations are not immutable and are modified in the heat of new and extreme situations, to which communities respond on the basis of a specific culture, history, and identity.

One specific example of this is the barter system carried out by the Kokonuko people, who in recent years have carried out more than sixty exchanges of agricultural products. In one barter market that took place on the Poblazón reservation in February of 2020, more than six hundred Indigenous people participated, most of them young people who defended a "clean economy in which barter is a rejection of neoliberalism and any monetary exchange."[21]

It is important to know that barter is much more than an economic practice here. These are exchanges of seeds and knowledge,

20.   Raúl Zibechi, "Los Pueblos En Movimiento," 233.
21.   Jóvenes CRIC, "Trueque Alto del Rey, Pueblo Kokonuko," video, August 2, 2022, https://www.youtube.com/watch?v=MemPUumqc3Q.

meetings where "our exercise of territorial, spiritual, economic, and social governance for the survival as Indigenous peoples" is put into play.[22] That is why barter fairs include Andean music, plays, dances, harmonization rituals, and "educational barter," with the aim of strengthening usos y costumbres, including the development of their own economy, self-justice, and ongoing reflections on their communal cultural practices: "Barter is now regarded as a strategy of resistance to the economic model that commodifies everything; it is a step toward food sovereignty, the integration of peoples and resistance," said the Nasa authorities years before the pandemic.[23]

Finally, the Nasa people have also begun to transform how they come to elect their authority figures. For several years, at least in northern Cauca, the traditional electoral practice of choosing by lists through a propaganda campaign has been abandoned. Instead, people are chosen with "spiritual" criteria. Each village proposes the person it considers most suitable according to the principles of the Nasa worldview and in an assembly where the cabildo elders choose the six or seven most suitable to occupy positions.[24]

A Community Market

CECOSESOLA, is the Spanish acronym for Cooperativa Central de Servicios Sociales del Estado Lara (The Central Cooperative for

22. Consejo Regional Indígena del Cauca (CRIC), "Primer Trueque de Semillas Propias e Intercambio de Productos en el Norte del Cauca," CRIC website, May 29, 2020, https://www.cric-colombia.org/portal/primer-trueque-de-semillas-propias-e-intercambio-de-productos-en-el-norte-del-cauca.

23. CRIC. "Trueque Comunitario Realizaron las Comunidades Indígenas de Corinto," Çxhab Wala Kiwe website, June 30, 2017, https://nasaacin.org/trueque-comunitario-realizaron-las-comunidades-indigenas-de-corinto.

24. Conversation with Berta Camprubí, December 9, 2020.

Social Services in Lara), a network of communities that extends across five northwestern states of Venezuela, with agricultural production, small-scale agro-industries, health services, transportation, funeral services, saving and loan capabilities, mutual aid funds, and distribution of food and household items.

There are just over twenty thousand associated members, of which thirteen hundred are workers who receive the same weekly "advance," as they call their salary. About four thousand participate in the more than three hundred annual meetings, between the weekly meetings and the *vivencias*, or extraordinary meetings of coexistence. In Lara's capital, Barquisimeto, which has just over one-million inhabitants, CECOSESOLA's three regularly scheduled fairs supply between 30 and 40 percent of fresh food for the community. At peak times there are 250 boxes that serve 55,000 families per week (about 200,000 people), with good quality products at a better price than on the open market. The Integral Cooperative Health Center (CICS), with which six neighborhood health centers are coordinated, serves 200,000 people annually and manages the largest funeral home in the region.

Altogether, the cooperatives make up a network of sixty grassroots cooperatives, ranging from 2,000 to 3,500 members each, with a wide variety of activities: from agricultural production, especially vegetables, honey, natural cosmetics, cleaning products, sauces, and sweets, among several other artisanal productions. Service and savings cooperatives are the ones with the most members in the region. The supply network has thirty sales spaces in four different states, including the three large, regularly scheduled fairs that mobilize five hundred tons of fruit and vegetables every week with annual sales of more than one hundred million dollars.

The point of providing this data is to show that these are not marginal enterprises, and CECOSESOLA has a significant weight in the regional economy. Before looking at how trade occurs between rural producers and points of sale, let's look at the criteria on which CECOSESOLA builds community.

To overcome what they consider to be a "tendency to parasitic complicity"—individualism, pandering, and leveling that dilutes differences and responsibilities—they decided to build bonds of trust that facilitated the creation of a community organization "where the power represented by their directive was diluted."[25] In order to do this, CECOSESOLA saw it was necessary to work intensely in medium-sized groups, avoiding large meetings in which the links were weakened. Toward the end of the 1990s things began to change: the disciplinary committees (which came from the period in which it was a union organization) ceased to be a necessity, and a more relaxed climate developed as part of a process of personal and organizational transformation. Over the years, directors and other hierarchies disappeared (which remain only in statutory form) with the creation of six meeting work committees: health, community production, fairs, services, cooperative management, and local planning. To these they later added meetings of mutual support, "educational coexistence" (which they give special attention), and general assemblies. Contrary to what happens in traditional organizations, there is a great turnover in the participants, which they visualize as something positive, to the extent that it allows them to "oxygenate" each space through the permanent renewal of its members.

Meetings are called so that members can avoid disputes over power. These meetings bear a resemblance to the traditional meetings of parties or unions, in which a "board of directors"—often

25. CECOSESOLA Escuela Cooperativa Rosario Arjona, *Buscando Una Convivencia Armónica* (Barquisimeto, Venezuela: CECOSESOLA, 2003), 25. Available at https://cecosesola.org/wp-content/uploads/2020/06/Buscando-una-Convivencia-Arm%C3%B3nica.pdf, accessed October 17, 2023.

sitting one step higher than the others—sets the agenda, establishes the quorum necessary in order to meet, themselves removed from the constituents. The CECOSESOLA meetings take up about 25 percent of the time members spend in the cooperatives, seeking a consensus that is achieved no matter how many hours or days are required to reach it. Sales are concentrated on Fridays, Saturdays, and Sundays, allowing associate workers time for meetings— four days to plan and discuss problems—and to participate in other areas.

The most novel aspect of their organization is the way the relationship between supply and demand works. The consumer and producer organizations spend three months planning the relationship between supply and demand. They then send the plan over to producers to adapt, reserving a time each week to hold open meetings to evaluate how the fairs have been working. The second difference with the market is that prices do not fluctuate but are fixed from production costs. In participatory processes, the so-called "cost meetings," in which the organization of the fairs participates with the producers, are carried out in order to ensure that "the calculations made by the different associations of participants are compared and the production costs for each item are established on a quarterly basis."[26] These price agreements are constantly discussed and reevaluated.

The third innovation is the single price per kilo they set for most of the fruit and vegetable products, a price that is updated every week based upon cost calculations and market prices, which they call "weighted price." In this way, the most expensive products are allowed to be subsidized by the products whose production prices are lower, and in addition there is no problem caused by the

---

26. Madeleine Richer and Ignacio Alzuru, "Intercooperación y Economía Solidaria: Análisis de Una Experiencia Venezolana," *Cuadernos de Desarrollo Rural* 1, no. 52 (2004): 111.

lack of demand for expensive products. Additionally, sales are more fluid since buyers fill their bags with the various products that have the same price and weigh them all together.

CECOSESOLA markets work with another set of rules and regulations, through joint and nonbureaucratic planning between supply and demand with the participation of all the stakeholders. In capitalism, the monopolies set the prices, with the greatest conceivable opacity. In the cooperatives of Barquisimeto, the historical and transparent tradition of the market is recovered as a place where the various actors come into contact in a horizontal and relatively egalitarian system.

Every week, a part of the population of Barquisimeto, more than fifty-five thousand families, and families from five other states in the northwestern region of Venezuela, choose to buy at fairs and not in supermarkets where products are more expensive, even though they may be better presented. These cooperatives have an additional advantageous dimension: they have led to the creation of their own identity, complemented by the communication and information activities they get to carry out in the healthy food fairs that often have live music and entertainment.

In the CECOSESOLA fairs there are no cameras or private guards, only "community surveillance," which consists of all those who participate in the fair and monitor its progress. The morning I participated in the downtown fair someone's shoes had been lost in the uproar that formed at the entrance. When the loudspeakers announced that someone's shoes had been lost, within a few minutes they were found. This is what happens even when wallets and valuables are lost. Despite the lack of surveillance, *fugas* (what capitalism calls "theft") are minimal, compared to the frequency it occurs at supermarkets—a rate about five times higher.

The same philosophy that allowed CECOSESOLA to become the main distributor of food in the region is applied in the Regional

Indigenous Council of Cauca in neighboring Colombia (CRIC). CRIC works in general medicine, pediatrics, gynecology, and twelve other specialties. They have clinical laboratories and ultrasound services that serve two hundred thousand people between members and nonmembers. The coordination is based on weekly open meetings in which the workers as well as the doctors of the health center participate, on an equal basis, in assemblies in which they must all wait their turn to speak: "Promoting the participation of physicians in meetings seeks to transform the doctor-patient relationship and open a space for dialogue between citizens and health professionals, in a sector of activity where traditionally the doctor occupies a dominant position."[27]

The experience of CECOSESOLA was built without any support from the State or private companies. This commitment to autonomy does mean that they have clashed with the Chavista or Madurista governments; they have avoided confrontation. If they can maintain forms of cooperation with the government or the municipal administration, they will accept it, but everything they build, including the health clinic, is done with their own resources.

While they participate in the market economy, certain characteristics redefine how they interact with it, including new kinds of relationships and links, transactions, and prices that are strictly regulated by the community. This way, no actor, neither the network of producers nor the management of the points of sale, can make decisions without consulting the others. Another definitive characteristic is transparency. The prices received by production cooperatives, as well as sales prices, are openly discussed, including input prices, transportation, and all variables that form the price. When they reach agreements, they are respected, and if a producer

27.   Richer and Alzuru, "Intercooperación y Economía Solidaria," 119.

chooses to sell outside the network because prices change and they seek a greater profit, he is immediately out of the network for having breached the agreements.

In this way, the role of intermediaries as nodes of capital accumulation is overcome, since transparency allows for a limit on profits, and at times goes beyond this to make sure that the price between purchase and sale are moderated, with surpluses turned over to the collectives to strengthen them. There is no accumulation, neither of power nor of money, and the logic of the law of value does not govern exchanges. Perhaps that is why I can attest to the ways in which the whole network has been fighting austerity. Of course, it is a collective experience that suffers the vicissitudes of a situation as difficult as the one Venezuela is experiencing, but no one ever said that the transition to a better world would be a cakewalk, free of problems.

Liberating the Market and Labor under Capitalism

In the various processes that are leading the Latin American movements, the most prominent that we can observe is the recovery of the means of production, in particular the land, which is now being worked in the most diverse ways: familial, cooperatively, and through different forms of collective work. The recovery of the means of production goes beyond the fact that formal property is communal, in the hands of families or collectives. Land, through its possession, is just the first step from which many movements begin to weave a wide network of community, productive, and distribution services, based on noncapitalist criteria.

This tendency, typical of Latin America, goes against the grain of certain strains of Marxist theory on development, according to which, under capitalism, only the expropriation of the producers can be expected. In the last three decades, other kinds of expropriations have taken place: millions of hectares have been recovered throughout the continent; more than four hundred factories have been recovered by workers in Argentina; around twelve thousand community aqueducts operate in Colombia. In addition to these expropriations, tens of thousands of popular and solidarity economic enterprises have risen up, including self-built territories in the urban peripheries that are resisting the logics of the system.

We are facing a popular countercurrent or trend born from below, which supposes the recovery of a part of what has been appropriated by capitalism. For Marx and Engels, and for a part of their followers, this expropriation played a positive role in history, because it freed the workers from their "bondage" to the means of production and turned them into wage earners. This has been part of the "revolutionary" role that the *Communist Manifesto* grants to the bourgeoisie in history. Engels explains it transparently in one of the polemics he takes up with anarchist thinker Pierre-Joseph Proudhon:

> In order to create the modern revolutionary class of the proletariat it was absolutely necessary to cut the umbilical cord which still bound the worker of the past to the land. The hand weaver who had his little house, garden and field along with his loom, was a quiet, contented man "in all godliness and respectability" despite all misery and despite all political pressure; he doffed his cap to the rich, to the priests and to the officials of the state; and inwardly was altogether a slave. It is precisely modern large-scale industry, which has turned the worker, formerly chained to the land, into a completely propertyless proletarian, liberated from all traditional fetters and free as a [jail-]bird; it is precisely this economic

revolution which has created the sole conditions under which the exploitation of the working class in its final form, in the capitalist mode of production, can be overthrown.[28]

According to this vision of progress and development, we in Latin America are seemingly facing exceptional processes of struggle that are piercing the bourgeois monopoly of ownership of the means of production as communities are building ways of life (production/reproduction and forms of power) controlled by societies in movement.

The landless peasants in Brazil and other parts of the continent are carrying out an agrarian reform from below, while other peasants are successfully determined to remain on their land in defiance of the arrogance of the multinationals and Marx's old assertion about "the idiocy of rural life." In our continent, the rural working classes are the ones who have launched the most powerful challenges to the domination of capital and neoliberalism.

This "anomaly" or "deviation" between theory and reality should lead us to question some foundational ideas of our critical thinking, converted over time into unappealable truths. This is not an argument for pragmatism but rather to place the reality of class struggles at the "helm" of our reflections. It happens that the "orthodox" way of reasoning, anchored in the European experience, has not undergone substantial changes despite the important anti-imperialist struggles in Vietnam and China, which led their leaders to theorizing that revolution consisted in elevating the status of the peasant.[29]

---

28. Frederick Engels, "The Housing Question," Marxists Internet Archive, https://www.marxists.org/archive/marx/works/1872/housing -question/cho1.htm.

29. Mao Tse-tung, "On New Democracy," Marxists Internet Archive, https://www.marxists.org/reference/archive/mao/selected-works/ volume-2/mswv2_26.htm.

The recovery of the means of production creates the material basis for a social conflict different from the ones carried out by organized workers—it provides a much greater strategic potential. The recovery of land, rural or urban, enables levels of autonomy that workers could never dream of. Not only do these peasant and marginalized movements recover land, but they work it in other ways, without the rigid division of labor between those who command and those who obey.

We see this take place in Brazil with the Landless Peasant Movement, a massive rural movement striving for land reform through occupation and new forms of social organizing. In the thousands of MST settlements, it is the assembles that decide what and how to produce, how the recovered lands are distributed (they can be family or private, collective or with various modes of cooperation) and also the channels through which production is distributed. The peasants' working hours are not dominated by a foreman that watches over them, they try not to cultivate with agro-toxins and have created a whole network of cooperatives and associations to produce, market, provide services, and credit cooperatives, or the so-called "popular banks." Each settlement decides what it does with its surpluses.

The Zapatistas created "anticapitalist" banks, such as Banpaz (Popular Autonomous Zapatista Bank) and Banamaz (The Autonomous Bank of Zapatistas). The decision to create them was taken in the assemblies of the communities, which also imposed very low interest rates, initially proposed to cover the health needs of families. Then they defined loans for collective projects, cooperatives, and societies with a higher interest rate although still comparatively low. While there are no loans for individual initiatives, loans are made available to individuals with personal needs.

The people are the ones who analyze each step to be taken and decide what suits them when considering a loan. Journalist Gloria

Muñoz recounts: "The endorsement of each applicant carries with it the authority of the community to which they belong, and the people remain as witnesses. In this way, the community is aware that one of their companions asked the bank for a little money and that he has to repay it."[30] This is why many Zapatista families no longer have to leave their communities to look for work in order to cover health expenses.

The initial funds from these banks came from several sources: contributions from the Zapatista Army of National Liberation; the profits of the collective transport administered by the Junta de Buen Gobierno; taxes that towns charged companies to build roads through their communities, and donations from their regional and global solidarity networks.

Communities manage money as a service to families and support bases, not as a business or means of accumulation. The money that circulates is collective property and is controlled by the assemblies so that it does not function as exchange value but rather as use-value. It is true that this mode challenges the principles of political economy, but I believe that these realities deserve to be analyzed and reflected upon. If communities control the circulation of funds, it ensures there is no private appropriation of the surpluses and that everything is used to improve collective life.

Something similar happens with the organization of work in a multitude of communities and popular undertakings. The assemblies decide the work to be done and how to do it, controlling the schedule without foremen or guards and they decide what is sold to the outside and how it is sold. Collective/community control of labor does not abolish the division of labor but subjects it to the will of the community, breaking the command/obedience scheme and

---

30. Gloria Muñoz Ramírez, "Insólito Banco Anticapitalista en la Selva Lacandona," *Desinformémonos*, March 5, 2012, https://desinformemonos .org/insolito-banco-anticapitalista-en-la-selva-lacandona.

absorbing the contradiction between intellectual and manual labor, the central aspects of capitalism.

The division between intellectual and manual labor often overlaps with similar command-obedience dynamics as decision makers are left out of the manual labor that is performed by those who receive orders. In the assembly, while we find all aspects of work coming into play, some individuals still remain entrenched in old ways, for example in the gendered division of labor in the traditional family. For this reason, the struggle against patriarchy plays a decisive role in this dismantling of the relations of production carried out by the collectives we call "societies in movement."

An argument used by those who dismiss these experiences is that work on the land is relatively simple and allows the contradiction and opposition between intellectual and manual labor to simply be moved around. However, in the Zapatista clinics the specialists (doctors and others) work with the direction of the communities, which do not allow them to use the privileges of knowledge for individualistic purposes. Among the landless peasants of Brazil, the technicians (agronomists, architects, and others) relate on an equal footing with the peasants. They jointly debate in the assemblies and meetings of work teams, exchanging opinions through a kind of connection that in no way supposes something similar to the oppositional command-obedience relationship that is more common in these types of spaces.

The doctors who work in the health spaces of CECOSESOLA tend to relate in a nonhierarchical but cooperative way with nurses and assistants, with administrative, maintenance, and service personnel. All of them use the same daily dining room and participate in a weekly assembly that meets in a large circle. These collective circles are responsible for managing the Comprehensive Community Health Center. During the pandemic, the communities came together to develop a network of trucks to transport people to clinics because of the difficulties presented by public transport. Altogether, medical power is slowly dismantled through the empowerment of communities into health groups. Although not all doctors in the region participate in these collective processes, it is an open path that can be deepened over time.

The Praxis of Resistance

Movements simultaneously resist and create. Resistance is part of all movements no matter when they occur. But something very particular is happening here in Latin America: the popular sectors no longer have a place of dignity and are instead subordinate in neoliberal societies in which the extractive model dominates. That is why the people need to create spaces where they can feel safe, where they are protected, spaces that are refuges that provide breathing room. This can only happen in territories that are community controlled and defended.

In these spaces they are able to create relationships that do not reproduce the hegemonic world but transform hierarchical and patriarchal relations, opening themselves to bonds of reciprocity and complementarity. These communities are also able to establish another kind of relationship with nature, land, and water, with other human and non-human beings. These are spaces where education and health do not work with the logic of the market but to empower people and peoples.

In the over two thousand schools in the settlements and camps of the MST, primary and adult literacy is carried out with their own pedagogy. Here, education is done differently than in the state system, because these are spaces built by the movement through collective work, with teachers who were born in and live in the agrarian reform settlements. Education is not limited to the classroom but extends its special interests to the outdoor spaces of the settlement and movement. Education in the MST is a process, rather than a thing, that puts the school in movement, so that the pedagogical instrument does not need to be a person, nor to be in school, nor be an institution.[31]

What is central to this idea of education is the social relations that the school deploys through its daily practice, much more than the content or the curriculum that it proposes. "The educational principal par excellence is in the movement itself, the process of *becoming*—the land, the people, the pedagogy itself—this being the root and the main format of its pedagogical identity."[32] That is why we say that the pedagogical instrument or teacher is movement itself as they are perpetually transforming. The depth of educational change is remarkable, to the point that the MST settlements defend "the pedagogical intentionality of each of the activities of the movement and not only those considered as undergoing education or training."[33]

We are facing a true revolution in the field of education, as alternatives to logocentric education are incorporated. The focus is no longer on the knowledge of the teacher in the school/institution, who acts as a "delegate" of a State at the service of capital. In short, it is not an education either for the benefit of capital or for the State but for the movement of transformation itself.

All forms of community self-defense and autonomous self-management simultaneously play practical social roles and an educational role in their movement. What can otherwise be read as a kind of praxis is a way of being that is not only expressed but

---

31. Roseli Salete Caldart, *Pedagogia do Movimento Sem Terra: Escola é Mais do Que Escola* (Petrópolis, Editora Vozes, 2000).
32. Caldart, *Pedagogia do Movimento Sem Terra*, 207.
33. Caldart, *Pedagogia do Movimento Sem Terra*, 249.

put into practice through the social movement, serving an educational role and strengthening the communities and the structures and material bases of the peoples who resist. We can see this in the way that many people who serve as facilitators or educators play significant roles in the defense of communities against mining, as is the case with the *Rondas Campesinas* of Cajamarca, which protects the headwaters of the rivers from the pollution left by multinational mining corporations.

This "other world" does not exist as a continuous whole but as islets that sometimes make up archipelagos of noncapitalist social practices, or they can be thought of as loose threads of a huge loom that pueblos are beginning to weave, while states and capital unweave them in many other ways, through welfare policies that create dependency, the installation of extractive companies in their territories, or through the State and parastatal repression found in narcostates. With regards to welfare, communities are rendered dependent subjects who forget how to steward land. This does not simply lead to material dependency but cultural and political need as well. As such, communities lose confidence in themselves, adopting the agenda of the State instead of their own.

The "other world" does not exist as an institution or in the form of the State but it does exist in the form of more or less extensive and permanent practices. These practices sometimes give life to their own "nonstate institutions," such as the good government juntas in Chiapas, the cabildos in Cauca, the bonfires in Cherán, the barricades in Oaxaca (that lasted for six months in 2006), the assemblies in the recovered factories, and in some of the most diverse ways of making decisions and enforcing them in many territories across Latin America.[34]

---

34. Raúl Zibechi, *Movimientos Sociales en América Latina: El Mundo Otro en Movimiento.* (Málaga: Bajo Tierras Ediciones, 2018).

What is common among these experiences is that both the production and reproduction of life, health and education, self-defense and self-justice, are woven as social relations emanating from grassroots organizations that, being the subjects of these processes and practices, use them to strengthen the collective. In order to move forward they must resist and fight one day at a time against a system that seeks to eliminate them because these communities are obstacles to their accumulation.

The descriptions laid out before you here would be incomplete without acknowledging that the MST and CRIC receive significant funds from the State and that the Zapatista territories are cordoned off by a large military deployment of the Mexican army and paramilitaries. In general, all of them are being harassed by the ultra-right governments and large multinational corporations. Just as Cuba suffers from a blockade, the territories of these movements are under daily attack and are subjected to strong economic and military pressures, as well as bad press. Therefore, in addition to "other worlds," these are worlds *in resistance* for their survival.

An Overview

At this point, it is necessary to define what exactly is meant by socialism and, above all, what social practices would be capable of propelling society toward new horizons? The great transition beyond capitalism has been thought of as a process that begins with the seizure of state power and the overthrow of the ruling classes. This transition would take time and the features of capitalism would survive, as well as the features of a society we might not ideally desire.

History teaches us that new social relations appear sporadically and often spontaneously. They have had random developments, some were institutionalized and later lost their renewing character; others were co-opted and deformed by political power; not just a few were seen as dangerous to revolutionary power when they were not under its control. There was no profound reflection on emerging social relations—from the soviets to popular communes and the immense variety of people's organizations—in these processes. Nor was there profound reflection on critical thinking as a whole, from the perspective of these experiences, and not from the perspective of the party/State.

What would it be like to think about socialism or the new world from the practices of autonomy and emancipation existing in these experiences and not from how they contribute—or don't—to the consolidation of power? The Russian experience has been the reference point for all the others. The Bolshevik party restricted the autonomy of the soviets, finding it to be a dangerous politic in the midst of civil war, something quite understandable indeed. Yet when the immediate dangers disappeared, the temptation to subordinate grassroots organizations took their course, and the Bolsheviks proceeded without backing down or reflecting on the costs that their decision would impose for the broader direction for the great transition. The same can be said about this kind of control over women's movements, dissident sexualities, peasants, and workers in general.

The former vice president of Bolivia, Álvaro García Linera, argues that the State should not and cannot be the driver of change, but should be the protective umbrella of popular innovation: "Socialism, as the construction of new economic relations, cannot be a state construction or an administrative decision."[35] Beyond his questionable conception of socialism as an economic system, he

---

35. Álvaro García Linera, "Qué es una Revolución?: De la Revolución Rusa a la Revolución de Nuestros Tiempos," in *Qué Es una Revolución? y Otros Ensayos Reunidos* (Buenos Aires: CLASCO, 2017), 222.

criticizes the idea that it is synonymous with the nationalization of the means of production and that that act is enough to build a society of a new kind.

His concept of transition is quite interesting for those of us concerned with critical thought. According to García Linera, the longer revolutionary power can hold, the longer it is possible to create "associative and community forms of production that spring from the voluntary experience of workers," among which includes the democratization of public service and cultural transformations, that is, the socialization of state functions.[36] He asserts that the State itself cannot create community "because it is the perfect antithesis of community," that it cannot invent communist social relations "because they only arise as autonomous social initiatives;" concluding that "if anyone has to build communism, it is society itself through its own self-organization and not through state directives."[37]

In short, in García Linera's opinion, the State must gain time so that society can deploy its emancipatory creativity that, necessarily, is born and develops in conflicts, struggles, failures, and new struggles. It is one of his main conclusions about the Russian Revolution, a century later. This is quite a radical departure from typical state-centric understandings of power; however, it was not what his government did while it was in power for fourteen years, in which time he came into conflict with Indigenous and popular organizations, which he repressed, dismantled, and co-opted. However, it is a pity that he has not stopped analyzing the profound forces that led to Stalin's rule and the counterrevolution he led. In some of his other texts, García Linera converges with Mao, although he does not make it explicit.

36. García Linera, "Qué es una Revolución?," 229.
37. García Linera, "Qué es una Revolución?," 229.

In fact, the Cultural Revolution maintained that the socialization of the means of production was not enough to march toward socialism, an issue that brought Maoist China to clash head-on with the prevailing ideas of the Communist Party in the Soviet Union. Mao had critiqued Stalin's book *Economic Problems of Socialism in the USSR*, stressing that the communist movement, that is, its politics and social mobilization, are the keys to the construction of the new society. "Chinese cadres participate in production; workers participate in management."[38]

Mao reached this conclusion after having understood the problems that the Soviet Union was going through, as he attempted to bridge the separation between its leadership and the rest of the people. Maoist politics, in words if not deeds, rejected hierarchies and defended the popular commune as the ideal organization to build socialism. He made this critical assertion of economism: "If there is no communist movement, it is impossible to pass to communism."[39] In short, communism places the class struggle on the most prominent plane: "In the course of a given period, the transformations of property systems always have a limit. But during the same period, human relations in production and labor can be constantly modified. With regard to the management of enterprises belonging to the whole people, we are in favor of a policy combining centralized leadership and mass movements, imposing party leadership, mixing workers and technical personnel, involving cadres in manual labor, continuously changing regulations and irrational systems, et cetera."[40]

---

38. Mao Tse-tung, "Concerning Economic Problems of Socialism in the USSR," Marxists Internet Archive, https://www.marxists.org/reference/archive/mao/selected-works/volume-8/mswv8_65.htm.

39. Mao Tse-tung, "Concerning Economic Problems."

40. Mao Tse-tung, "Notas de lectura del *Manual de Economía Política* de la Unión Soviética," in *La Construcción del Socialismo en China* (Córdoba: Cuadernos de Pasado y Presente, 1976), 106.

However, it should be noted that we do not have an in-depth analysis of the causes of the failure of the Cultural Revolution in China and the subsequent triumph of a capitalist-oriented economy. The dominant narratives usually attribute it to personal leadership, such as that of Stalin or Mao, Yeltsin or Deng Xiaoping, to explain the drifts that took these societies away from the road to socialism.

In what follows, I try to make sense of the practical shortcomings of García Linera and Mao by laying out three issues that have not been at the center of discussions but are of great importance. My intention is to open up debates and reflections:

Reproducing Coercive Power

Sociologist Immanuel Wallerstein argued that a transition *controlled and directed* by some entity, such as the party or the State, can reproduce the problems they intend to avoid. "A transition that is controlled, that is organized, is bound to involve some continuity of exploitation. We must lose our fear of a transition that takes the form of crumbling, of disintegration. Disintegration is messy, it may be somewhat anarchic, but it is not necessarily disastrous. 'Revolutions' may in fact be 'revolutionary' only to the degree they promote such crumbling. Organizations may be essential to break the crust initially. It is doubtful they can actually build the new society."[41]

The theme Wallerstein intends to highlight here is with regards to the continuities that persist in periods of transition. Those who direct and control the transition from above become a collection of people who have more power and influence in decision making than the rest of society. As is known, on this subject there have been

---

41. Immanuel Wallerstein, "Marx and Underdevlopment," in *Unthinking Social Science: The Limits of Nineteenth-Century Paradigms* (Cambridge: Polity Press, 1991), 169.

several interpretations coming from leftist projects from across the globe.

It seems necessary to reflect on the experiences of the socialist transition from nearly a century, fertilized by the history of previous transitions such as that of fiefdom to capitalism. It can be pointed out that transitions are lengthy processes, centuries rather than years, with marches and countermarches, and turning points, like revolutions. This is truer today given the systemic and civilizational crisis that is been accelerated by the pandemic.

On the characterization of post-revolutionary societies and the groups that exercise political power, we have a range of interpretations. In addition to those who argue that the leaderships of the parties in power embody the will of the working class and must be considered revolutionary, we count on the analysis of the Maoists, on the one hand, and of Trotsky's supporters, on the other.

For Charles Bettelheim, a leading French Marxian economist and the leaders of the Communist Party of China, the Soviet leadership had become a new bourgeoisie. The bibliography on the Cultural Revolution confirms this. For the French intellectual, a "state bourgeoisie" arose in the USSR within the framework of a "state capitalism." Part of the old bourgeoisie penetrated the administrative and economic apparatuses of the Soviet State while "relations of distribution" were developed that favored the party leaders and highly qualified specialists, so that "part of the surplus value produced in industry was thus appropriated by this new bourgeoisie."[42]

The Trotskyist current, for its part, insisted on considering the USSR a "bureaucratized workers' state," rather than a class society. Therefore a political revolution would overthrow the Stalinist

---

42. Charles Bettelheim, *Class Struggles in the USSR: First Period, 1917–1923* (New York: Monthly Review, 1976), 164.

leadership and restore workers' and people's power, but it would not be a revolution of a social character, since the means of production remain in the hands of the State.[43] According to this current, one of the main reasons for the advent of the bureaucracy is that the revolution has not spread to other countries, which forced it to build socialism in a single country.

It is not the case of taking sides with any of these interpretations but to emphasize the difficulties that the Marxist camp has had, and continues to have, in dialoguing and deepening its understanding of these problems. This is of critical importance especially since the new generations of militants are unaware of those intense debates that took place in the 1960s and 1970s. I think it is convenient to devise some general hypothesis about the transition, although it should not be so detailed as to generate doctrine that cannot incorporate novelties and those popular creations that, apparently, move beyond a pre-established script.

The Site of Revolution

The second issue I would like to discuss is the fact that it is often taken for granted that the revolution should take place in a nation-state, something that seems like a logical inference given that revolutions revolve around the conquest of state power. Therefore, the scale of the transition is that of the nation-state, which, as a whole or totality, must transition into a new society, new economy, and new culture. New social relations must be built within that totality, without consideration for uneven development, by which I mean the presence of societies that have chosen other "development" paths other than the hegemonic ones, either because of subjugation or their own free will. Nor for the fact that in certain

---

43. Ernest Mandel, *Power and Money: A Marxist Theory of Bureaucracy* (New York: Verso, 1992).

limited spaces, and with appropriate conditions and social will, this uneven development can be replicated.

On this point, I would like to introduce the thought of the historian Fernand Braudel. The historical research to which he devoted his life led him to a thesis that departed from the general consensus that understood the succession of modes of production (slavery, feudalism, capitalism, and communism) and the homogeneity of capitalism as central tenets of critical thought.

Braudel argues that capitalism is the child of never-ending growth, without which it could not have prospered or created the great inequality of the world. The expansion of the world-system of the initial European framework across the planet where the "conquest" of America played a fundamental role, was what made it possible for capitalist practices that existed for a long time to be deployed with all their potential: "Capitalism is the son of the authoritarian organization of an obviously excessive space. It would not have grown with such force in a limited economic space."[44]

On the other hand, Braudel argues that society is made up of three floors: material life, the market economy, and capitalism or the countermarket. The first is the space that is defined by daily life, the routine of the nuclear family, and its self-contained consumption, where use-value predominates and that always was, and continues to be, a very wide space in our societies. The second, economic life or the market economy, is the place of exchanges, always regulated in history to prevent the few from taking advantage of the many.

The typical character of material life is the peasant who sells some products in the market, who "touches only the limit of the market"; while the merchant is inserted in the market economy,

---

44. Fernand Braudel, *La Dinámica del Capitalismo* (Madrid: Alianza, 1985), 95.

dominated by the great merchants who overlap a huge mass of small merchants. In our continuum, the enormous mass of "informality" is part of the "market economy."

But capitalism is somewhat different: "Above the enormous mass of daily material life, the market economy has laid its nets and kept alive its various fabrics. And it was, ordinarily, above the market economy itself that capitalism thrived."[45] In short, household consumption and exchange were at this point not yet capitalism. Markets are "regular, predictable, routine, and open to both small and large traders," because in them trade is "regulated, fair, and transparent," that is, it is subject to control.[46]

That is why Braudel defines capitalism as the "countermarket," the place of unequal exchanges where monopolies not competition works, "where the great predators prowl and the law of the jungle rules," because it moves at a distance from the real market and material life, breaks the relations between the producer and the final recipient of the commodities. In this way it escapes the rules and controls, moves "long distance" and achieves "abnormal benefits." Monopolies succeed in nullifying competition and installing the opacity of economic linkages. The capitalist does not specialize in anything as he is the "night visitor," the bird of prey that parasitizes material life and the market economy and that to succeed needs to ally with the prince: "Capitalism only triumphs when it identifies with the State, when it is the State."[47]

Throughout his work, Braudel emphasizes that capitalism is power, not economics, an idea later developed by the Kurdish leader Abdullah Öcalan. Noncapitalist or new types of social relations can only arise in the vast ocean of material life, which may then spread to the world of exchanges or economic life. That is where

---

45. Braudel, *La Dinámica del Capitalismo*, 45.
46. Braudel, *La Dinámica del Capitalismo*, 54–55.
47. Braudel, *La Dinámica del Capitalismo*, 68.

the non-capitalist practices of Latin American social movements emerged: in spaces controlled by the people, where monopolies have no access. It is in these sheltered spaces, at a distance from capitalism, where the new societies can emerge.

At the end of his extensive work, *Afterthoughts on Material Civilization and Capitalism*, Braudel critiques Soviet thought and Lenin. He considered that, in its daily practice, small commodity production gives rise spontaneously to capitalism and the bourgeoisie. Capitalism began for Lenin in the village market. The obvious conclusion is that "to get rid of capitalism, it is necessary to root out individual production and freedom of exchange," Braudel reasons. This position does not take into account "the enormous creative power of the market," of the lower zone of trade, crafts and "unusual activities."[48]

The antisystemic struggle in our world is anchored in material life and the market economy. This is where resistance and innovation take place, in the space that Braudel calls "the ground floor" of societies. It is there that the settlements and camps of the MST in Brazil; the cabildos and the Nasa community enterprises in Cauca, Colombia; and the good government juntas in Chiapas operate; as well as the set of resistances and the creations of new social relations.

I conclude this section by pointing out that when the ruling class has been removed from state power, the attention of revolutionary changes and transition is fixed precisely on the ground floor of societies.

Socialism and Power

Socialism, or the transitional society, is the power of the workers. It has nothing to do with the development of the productive

---

48. Fernand Braudel, *Perspective of the World* (London: William Collins Sons & Co, 1984), 631.

forces, as a certain economistic Marxism has claimed. Socialism is not concerned with the elimination of commercial activities or the circulation of money (which, while not centered in socialism, is believed to be an entity that should be regulated). The recovery of media production and exchange is a fundamental prerequisite of socialism, but it is insufficient.

In historical experiences, save for some brief periods, power has been exercised—in countries where revolutions took place—in the name of the workers (peasants, workers, professionals, etc.) but not by them directly. That is why I believe that the central aspect of the new society is self-governance at all levels of the popular sectors: in communities and *ejidos* (state-supported communal farms in Mexico), in municipalities and rural and urban territories. The new world can take the form of a vast network of local self-governments connected to each other through nonhierarchical forms or, even better, hierarchies under the control of autonomous governments.

The day-to-day functioning of the Zapatista juntas de buen gobierno, which administer territories populated by tens of thousands of people, rotate the government team composed of up to twenty-five people once a week. The three levels of autonomy— *ejidos*, towns or communities, municipalities and regions—are governed by the criterion of the greatest possible participation in decision making, even on more complex issues such as the process of imparting justice.

The network of local self-government is probably the most appropriate picture of the kind of society we seek, as opposed to a centralized State that has in its hands not only a monopoly on legitimate violence but on the whole of the means of production and exchange. This State will have overwhelming power over society where a new ruling class makes up its nucleus. No longer is the center composed of the owners of capital, who no longer exist. The center of the socialist State is composed of the managers or administrators installed at the top of the State apparatus.

A power that manages to "institute, in a lasting way, the monopoly of coercion, taxes, public education, the liturgy of power and political-cultural legitimacy," that is, "the constitution of a revolutionary state that monopolizes decisions to the detriment of dispersed and weak social democratism" ends up being—as I think historical experience has shown—an end in itself.[49] Although García Linera defends the idea of a concentrated and decentralized State against the old dominant classes pitted against the workers, in reality the inertia and the political culture that emanates from the exercise of such power end up weighing down the best intentions of social transformation.

If we think that capitalism is an economy or that the law of value is the core of capitalism, argues García Linera, we will reason that socialism is also an economy. But if we consider capitalism to be power (as Öcalan does), then the core of socialism is social and class struggle. "If really all take part in the administration of the state, capitalism cannot retain its hold," writes Lenin in *The State and Revolution*. From the moment the armed people take the management of the State into their own hands, or at least the immense majority of the workers do so, "need for a special machine of suppression will begin to disappear."[50] It is exactly the image we have of the juntas of good governance and the network of Zapatista powers, which I have chosen to call "nonstate powers."[51]

Therefore, at the core of socialism we find concrete direction of concrete affairs, neither a mode of production nor the economy in

49. García, "Qué es una Revolución?," 97, 52.
50. V. I. Lenin, "The State and Revolution," in *Collected Works*, vol. 25 (Moscow: Progress Publishers, 1964), 468.
51. Raúl Zibechi, *Descolonizar: El Pensamiento Crítico y las Prácticas Emancipatorias* (Montevideo: Alter ediciones, 2020).

its broadest sense. As we know, in the Soviet experience the management of enterprises fell to a director, just as the higher commands of the armed forces were professionalized, and so on across all aspects of life in society. This goes in the opposite direction of socialism, reproducing capitalist logics with the argument of efficiency.

Finally, a question to conclude this intervention. How do the social struggles of our current period, in particular feminist and Indigenous peoples' moments, affect our understanding of capitalism and its oppressions, of revolution and of the new world we wish to build?

The struggle of women and Indigenous peoples has transformed my conception of capitalism, of the forms of struggle and of the type of society that is possible. Today we understand the importance of patriarchy and colonialism as two central axes in capitalist domination, because feminist, Black, and Indigenous struggles have managed to make visible the oppressions that were naturalized under this system. But it is through the activism of these collective subjects, in addition to them exposing these oppressions, that tells us they want to govern themselves and that they are not willing to cede control over their lives to others, even to those that say all the right things and have the best intentions.

❋ ❋ ❋

To conclude, I would like to point out that the traditions that influence antisystemic movements are a plurality of sorts, that is, they are not inscribed exclusively in the Western emancipatory tradition but, significantly, in the Indigenous and popular Latin American revolutionary traditions. The Marxist, anarchist, and social democratic Western traditions are part of a rational paradigm, in tune with the Enlightenment, centered on the concept of citizenship and individual human rights. Unlike Creole-led processes,

Indigenous peoples have been inspired by their own traditions. The Pan-Andean revolutions of 1780 led by Túpac Amaru and especially by Túpac Katari, were inspired neither by the French nor the Haitian revolution and belong to another genealogy than the processes that promoted Creole independence. The rebels of 1780 based their demands and actions on their communal traditions and as peoples, on the assembly, decentralized practices, and on the traditional system of rotating or turn-based positions.[52]

I mean that there is a rebellious and emancipatory genealogy that is neither enlightened nor rationalist, and though it has not been granted attention from academies and left-wing parties, is at the root of the "other" thought and practices of a substantial portion of the oppressed pueblos of Latin America. These *otherwise* genealogies are reflected in some way in the concepts of *sumak kawsay* (good living) or *suma qamaña* (living well), which the Ecuadorian Kwichuas and the Bolivian Aymaras and Quechuas have incorporated into the new constitutions. "Limpid and harmonious life," that is, to live in such a way as to establish a harmonious relationship between human beings and, therefore, between them and nature, since there is no difference between the way people relate to one another and how they relate with the space in which they live.

It is a radical break from Western culture, with the ideas of progress and development, with the proposals of unlimited growth and consumption that are nothing more than the perpetual accumulation of capital and power in a stratified society. But it is also a break with modernity, with colonialism and Eurocentrism. The civilizational crisis we are experiencing suggests that the analytical instruments we have to understand and analyze reality are no longer reliable. They are knowledges born of a colonial matrix (such as the

52. Sinclair Thomson and Silvia Rivera Cusicanqui, *Cuando Sólo Reinasen Los Indios: La Política Aymara En La Era de La Insurgencia* (La Paz: Muela del Diablo, 2006).

subject-object relationship on which they are based) and are limited to consecrating the current civilizational pattern as something natural, preventing different ways of living from flourishing. *Vivir bien* or buen vivir is an art guided by principles and an alternative way of living in the face of the civilization of death, not a list of demands that can be formulated as rights of citizens and duties of States. An art that supposes harmony with nature, considered as a mother on which we depend and with which we cannot establish a relationship of competition or domination.

In the urban-popular sectors, there are many cultures that operate independently from the hegemonic one. These alternative cultures have a strong influence on urban movements, which is evident in their varied approaches, ranging from Argentine slum priests to more academic analyses of Venezuelan popular neighborhoods. These popular sectors have long signified the existence of an urban culture based on a powerful sociability, anchored in being or "*estar-ser*" (becoming) where social relationality is determined and capable of shaping a world of popular life with characteristics very different from the hegemonic society, including economic relations outside the market.

Indigenous traditions together with the urban-popular ones, of which the Afro-descendant, rural, and religious bases are also a part, make up a set of ethical and symbolic references. These form values based on usos y costumbres and can be found in many antisystemic movements. It is not that there is a similar emancipatory paradigm elsewhere but that there are numerous different kinds of paradigms than that of the West: a substratum of rebellious traditions, multiple and unified, practiced and not theorized, which are feeding the ways and forms of today's insubordinate movements. Of course, the movements inspired by these traditions do not exclude those that the antisystemic movements have inherited from the French Revolution and subsequent revolutions but enrich them just as they are, on some occasions, working through and with the politics presented by Western/northern proposals. Such is the case of women's liberation, where feminist collectives have contended with dominant liberal paradigms and those from the everyday, a tension that is not present in either Indigenous Latin American or urban-popular traditions.

On the contrary, in these spaces there is nothing like the *tabula rasa* inherited from the Enlightenment, or the separation between theory and action, or even between strategy and tactics, since in these original/Indigenous cultures there is no division between means and ends.

The three aspects I mentioned in this section allow us to debate the concept of social movements that emanate from the Eurocentric way of understanding. In the central countries, social and anti-systemic movements act within a society that they seek to change, and their debates have focused on how to achieve the objectives proposed, as well as on the forms of action and organization. In Latin America we can observe that antisystemic movements are beginning to turn their spaces into alternatives to the dominant system for two reasons: they turn them into simultaneous spaces of survival and political action, and they build noncapitalist social relations in them. The way they take care of health, educate them-selves, and the way they produce their food and distribute it, is not mere reproduction of the capitalist pattern but—in a considerable part of these enterprises—we see an effort to go further, to question all aspects in the inherited ways of doing.

We can observe then that in Latin America there is not "one" society but two, more or less separated and differentiated, in whose formation the colonial fact seems to have played a decisive role. It is in this fracture where the most important antisystemic movements are acting. The territorial control they exercise has been the key to their creating small worlds of social relations against capitalists and nonstate powers within the realm of the oppressed. These movements from below have come a long way in the last five centuries: from the reappropriation of land and space to the creation of territories; from the creation of new subjectivities to the constitution of new and different political subjects with respect to the old unionized industrial working class and the parties that represented it; from unemployment to the creation of new trades making way for rebellious economies. This long process has not, in my opinion, been reflected in all its complexity and we have not yet discovered all its potentialities.

The central aspect of this debate is whether or not there is indeed a system of social relations that are expressed or condensed within a territory. This means entering the analysis of movements from another place: no longer the forms of organization and the repertoires of mobilization but social relations, territories, and the reappropriation of the means of production. In this type of analysis, new concepts such as autonomy, community, nonstate powers (among the most prominent) will appear. Latin American antisystemic movements pose both the overcoming/destruction of capitalism and nation states, and an equally important battle for the decolonization of thought and in particular, critical thinking. In this sense, the concepts of social movements and even antisystemic movements could be complemented with proposals and debates that have been born in the heat of the latest wave of social struggles, such as "societal movements" or "societies in movement." Both concepts seek to account for the fact that, during the last decade, social relations have changed from those hegemonized by capital and States; that is, not only has a part of society been mobilized, but a different society, interwoven by noncapitalist social relations, has been on the move.

This implies modifying our inherited assumptions about revolution and social change. Or, better yet, to recover some of the most brilliant insights of the founders of socialism, such as the one outlined by Marx in his report on the Paris Commune. The changes are produced by antisystemic movements, but not simply because they modify the balance of forces in society—which modify it in fact and in turn—but because in them forms are born, grow, and germinate into social bonds that are the mortar of the new world. No longer "the" new world but outgrowths of that world.

Marx asserted that the workers do not have prefabricated utopias to put into practice, nor do they have to realize their ideals but "give way" to the elements of the new society that the old bourgeois society carries within it. His concept of revolution as the midwife of history goes in that same direction.

This "other" world already exists in some way within many antisystemic movements. Proof of this is the juntas de buen gobierno in Chiapas, the landless settlements in Brazil, and the hundreds of factories recovered by their workers, to mention just a few cases. Apparently, a part of the Latin American movements, as Subcomandante Insurgente Marcos has pointed out, would be trying a new way of doing politics from below, outside the state institutions that they no longer intend to occupy—though they continue to aspire to destroy, in order to (in line with Marx) "unleash" (expand, spread) the new world that already beats in the heart of the movements.

Cauca's Indigenous Guard
Engines of Care and Transformative Change

Y seguiremos peleando mientras no se apague el sol
(We continue to fight as long as the sun does not go out)
—PÁEZ/NASA PEOPLES' ANTHEM

Its June 2008 in the village of El Damián, Tacueyó reservation, in the central cordillera of the department of Cauca in Colombia.[1] At the bottom of a deep hollow, the Palo River collects the waters that come down from the mountains. From its almost perpendicular slopes the peasant crops of bananas, coffee, cassava, beans, potatoes, and corn become the setting for loud scrimmages. Since mid-March, fighting between the Revolutionary Armed Forces of Colombia (FARC) guerrillas and the army has been taking place at the highest point of the mountain. Soldiers there blew up a warehouse containing the guerrilla army's explosives, causing the death of a member of the Nasa Indigenous community and wounding fourteen. They went on to demolish all the houses within a radius of more than one hundred meters: the eight hundred residents of the two neighboring villages, El Damián and La María, took refuge in the rural school chosen as the place of "permanent assembly," the

---

1.   This work benefited from the contributions of Berta Camprubí and Didier Chirimuscay, communicators living in the Indigenous territory of Cauca, whom I thank for their invaluable collaboration.

preassigned meeting center in case of emergency. Above the school, a gigantic white flag tied over a very long cane was set up to dissuade the armed forces. More than half of the people are children, the rest mothers and elderly folks.

In Colombia, 2.5 percent of the population are Indigenous people scattered throughout the country. They speak more than sixty languages and are grouped into 670 reservations. Cauca is the department that presents the greatest geographical and cultural diversity, its territory borders the Pacific Ocean, and much of it integrates the Central Mountain Range, where most of the Indigenous people live. There are also many people present in the Colombian Massif, cradle of the great rivers of the country, in particular the Magdalena, the Cauca, and the Caquetá. There, 22 percent of the population is Indigenous, with another 22 percent being Afro-descendant and the rest mestizo or white.

The Defense of Life and Community

The multicolored mobilizations of the Nasa people in the mountains of the Colombian Cauca are carried out with a cordon of guards who are arranged to protect the *comuneros* and *comuneras*, in linear formation in front and on the sides, disciplinarily "armed" with batons of command, wooden sticks with the symbols of their ancestors. The protection and defense of communities is the objective of the Indigenous Guard, which considers itself both an educational and also a political entity in training.

Every year there is a graduation ceremony for hundreds of Guards in northern Cauca (southern Colombia). Men, women, and young people between twelve and fifty years old have at this point gone through the School of Political and Organizational Training where they train in modern human rights as well as in the "original law" to carry out their tasks. The graduation is an act of deep mystical practices, taking place in an atmosphere of harmony, guided by the wise elders of the communities who come together with university professors and human rights defenders.[2]

The structure of the Indigenous Guard is simple and shows what their organization is all about: each village (community) elects ten Guards and a coordinator in their assembly. A coordinator is then elected per reservation (Indigenous territory) and another for the entire region. In northern Cauca there are thirty-five hundred Indigenous Guard corresponding to eighteen cabildos (elected authorities in the reservations).[3]

"We have nothing to do with the police, we are trained in organization, we are invested in the protection of the community and defense of life without getting involved in the war," explains one of the coordinators of the Indigenous Guard.[4] Participation in the Indigenous Guard is voluntary and unpaid, the neighbors of the village and the authorities collaborate in the maintenance of the family garden of each chosen Guard and sometimes do mingas of sowing and harvesting.

Guards are evaluated once a year and can be kept on or replaced by others, as their organization is based on the rotation of all its members. Community justice—the central task of the Indigenous Guard—seeks to recover harmony and internal balances based on the Nasa worldview and culture. This differs from state-centered justice, which imprisons those who commit crimes,

2. Consejo Regional Indígena del Cauca (CRIC), "Caminates y Cuidadores Del Territorio," video, March 23, 2017, https://www.youtube .com/watch?v=PTrb7zZX5lc.
3. "Cabildos" refers to both authority figures and a semi-autonomous political organization of Indigenous communities in Colombia.
4. Raúl Zibechi, "Autoprotección Indígena contera la Guerra," April 19, 2008, Latin American Information Agency (online archive), https:// www.alai- net.org/es/active/23367.

separating them from their communities. The Guard defends the territory from the military, paramilitaries, and guerrillas who have killed and kidnapped hundreds of community members during the internal conflict.[5] In recent years, they have been protecting their territories from the mining carried out by multinationals, which pollutes and displaces populations.

In addition to advocating for the formation of councils and the organization of communities, Guard members encourage food sovereignty, promote community gardens, and encourage assemblies to reflect upon their self-derived "rights" as they call community justice. Every six months the Guards participate in rituals and ceremonies of harmonization. These ceremonies of harmonization speak to the processes bringing back social and cultural equilibrium between the human and nonhuman world, which sickness and violence has ruptured. These ceremonies are guided by traditional doctors as a form of individual and collective "cleansing."[6]

Peaceful resistance is one of the hallmarks of the Indigenous Guard. On several occasions, hundreds of its members have gathered in response to the community summoning them to rescue prisoners kidnapped by narco-paramilitaries or guerrilla forces. They make use of their large numbers of disciplined and determined Guards to free the hostages without violence. On occasion, they have also confronted the armed forces of the State.[7]

Today, the Indigenous Guard accompanies the community members, following the instructions of the Association of Indigenous Councils of Northern Cauca (ACIN), which states in

---

5. The internal conflict refers to the decades-long civil war in Colombia whose most notable combatants have been the State, paramilitary forces, and the Revolutionary Armed Forces of Colombia (FARC).
6. Throughout the Andean civilizations, the notion of equilibrium is central to local cosmologies.
7. Raúl Zibechi, "Autoprotección colectiva, dignidad y autonomía," *Contrapunto* 4 (May 2017).

a booklet that in cases of emergencies the population must go to spaces of "Indigenous resistance defined in assembly, spaces for protection, reflection, and community analysis," to resist together "respecting diversity and difference, so that the land of the future may be a fabric of collective consciousness and autonomy in balance and harmony with all beings of life."[8]

The coordinator of the Guards of the region, Luis Alberto Mensa, who is forty-two, carries a baton as the only sign of his authority, as do the other Guards who accompany him. As we toured the conflict zone, he explains that "the guard, which has always existed among the Nasa, became officially visible in 2001 as a result of a series of conflicts. People here did not believe that the armed conflict would reach this region because this was a historic zone of the FARC, but the paramilitaries entered and killed many people and the assemblies decided to install permanent Guards." To defend the territory, the Guards do not use weapons but instead promote training and organization to promote self-defense in the communities. Their strategies of resistance include promoting food sovereignty, early warnings, community gardens, and, above all, training processes, including permanent assemblies of reflection and decision making, all of which come together under the strengthening of the law and of their own authorities.

In 2004, the Indigenous Guard received the National Peace Prize, an award whose recipients have included a number of larger and internationally influential institutions, including the United Nations and the Friedrich Ebert Foundation. The Guard has become a reference for other peoples, such as Afro-descendants in the country, and also for peasants and popular sectors that suffer State or private violence in urban areas.

---

8. Raúl Zibechi, "Colombia: Autoprotección Indígena Contra La Guerra," Servicios de Comunicación Intercultural (Servindi) website, April 10, 2008, https://www.servindi.org/node/42833.

The Radical Ambiguity of the Nasa World

I propose to reflect on this as the radical ambiguity of the Colombian Indigenous movement, as it crosses all its manifestations, its organizational structures, and limits the enormous creative power of the movement, specifically by highlighting an incident surrounding the cultivation of the coca leaf. The main point of this case is not the coca leaf but the dependence on capitalism and the State, which pervades the entire Indigenous movement in Cauca, putting stress on the movement but not setting its conditions. Nevertheless, this dependency on capitalism and the State tests the emancipatory potential of the movement itself.

The murderers of the Indigenous governor Sandra Liliana Peña Chocué were sentenced to sixty years in prison. The decision was made at a multidisciplinary assembly in the village of Siberia, in the Sath Tama Kiwe area, where the 127 Indigenous authorities, associations, and the Chief Council of the CRIC presided as judges. The public hearing sentenced the two responsible for the murder of "mayora" Sandra Liliana, governor of the community of La Laguna-Siberia, municipality of Caldono, "to spend 60 years in prison without any judicial benefit." The assembly decided to destroy the weapons and material seized by state authorities and the Indigenous Guard during the investigation.[9]

The two who were convicted, who were themselves Indigenous, acknowledged their crime during the hearing and were found guilty of disharmonizing the territory and the community, of being involved with drug trafficking and armed groups. In the

---

9.   Consejo Regional Indígena del Cauca (CRIC), "60 años de Cárcel para Asesinos de la Gobernadora Indígena Sandra Peña Chocué," CRIC website, April 30, 2021, https://www.cric-colombia.org/portal /60-anos-de-carcel-para-asesinos-de-la-gobernadora-indigena-sandra -pena-chocue.

assembly's resolution, not only was the murdered person declared a victim but also her family, the community of the La Laguna Indigenous reservation, the autonomous government, the physical and cultural survival of the Nasa people, and the Indigenous organizational process.

The assassins said they were paid ten million pesos to kill the governor on April 20, 2021, of which five million pesos were received from gangs involved in drug trafficking. Members of the community say Sandra Liliana was murdered "for territorial control, to clear the territory, and to use Mother Earth for crops that today only bring death and desolation." Governor Sandra Liliana was known for her political clarity in the internal mingas, which led her to work to oppose the illicit transformation of the ancestral coca leaf into a monocultural production, ultimately leading to her assassination.

The convicted men were handed over to the Attorney General's office for later confinement in the San Isidro penitentiary, located in Popayán, in an agreement with the State known as "borrowed yard." The Colombian State lends the Indigenous authority its facilities so that Indigenous community members can serve their sentence. This modality emerged in 1999, when Indigenous authorities decided to resort to the prisons of the National Penitentiary and Prison Institute (INPEC) to enforce sentences imposed in the Indigenous "restorative justice" framework.[10]

Traditionally, the Nasa authorities and other Indigenous peoples that make up the CRIC are guided by the precepts of harmony and balance between people and nature. When someone breaks these "principles of life," they seek to recover harmony through certain spiritual practices or "remedies," but given the increase in serious cases (rapes and murders), they decided to utilize INPEC

---

10. María Socorro Granda Abella, "El 'Patio Prestado' Frente a Los Principios de La Justicia Restaurativa," *Revista Criterio Libre Jurídico* 8, no. 2 (July–December 2011).

prisons. Between 2005 and 2010 there were an average of 653 Indigenous people imprisoned in any given year, of which 28 percent were of the Nasa people. The crimes with the highest incidence here include homicide and assault.

Justicia propia (sovereign justice) with its ancestral authorities, norms, and procedures was incorporated into the 1991 Constitution, and recognized Colombia as a multiethnic and multicultural State. The problem I want to highlight here is that the Nasa people are a major entity of the CRIC that shows "the contradiction between worldview and practice in the exercise of sovereign justice."[11] This situation illustrates, like the others that appear throughout this essay, the radical ambiguity of the Indigenous world of Cauca: they build autonomous institutions all the while utilizing state resources; they assume their own forms in education and health but often rely on financing by the State for certain projects. The contradictions can be further widened, since illicit crops abound in the Indigenous reservations, so the presence of armed groups (from FARC dissidents to drug traffickers and paramilitaries) is common and the Indigenous Guard finds it extremely difficult to limit them.

In the dominant or hegemonic thought, greatly influenced by binary thinking (male/female, negative/positive, etc.), no room exists for blurred, mixed, or *mestizo* identities. For instance, during the colonial period, the viceregencies saw mixed populations as an anomaly, as something negative or deficient. Against binary thinking, I approach these autonomous movements with the understanding that nothing exists in a pure or essential form, that is, an absolutely pure society or anti-state movement. Many if not all of these movements, save for the Zapatistas, are in relation to the State, even though they consider themselves to be autonomous. Their autonomy is not so much in their relationship or lack thereof

---

11.   Granda Abella, "El 'Patio Prestado,'" 49.

with the State, but rather because they rearrange the resources of the State to better provide for themselves.

The CRIC and the Indigenous Guard

A seven-point program serves as the foundation for the CRIC: 1) recover the land of the reservations, 2) expand them, 3) strengthen the Indigenous councils, 4) do not pay for land, 5) make the laws for Indigenous people and demand they be applied, 6) defend Indigenous history, language, and customs, and 7) train Indigenous teachers "to educate according to the situation of the Indigenous people in their respective languages."[12]

The CRIC was born in 1971 in a massive assembly of two thousand delegates from seven councils and as many reservations. They came together to elect an executive committee that initially could not function due to the repression of the landowners. It was not until its second congress in September of that year that it was able to formulate its program. CRIC has a structure similar to the governing models of schools. Its administrative body, which is renewed every two years, defines it as a "collective of leaders chosen by the communities themselves who are elected through a regional assembly."

CRIC has adopted three major projects—political, economic, and cultural—that supplement programs in the areas of education, health, training, legal, communications, production, cooperatives, and revolving startup funds. CRIC relies on five transversal axes: Indigenous women, young people, traditional medicine, land, and environment. The various tiers of the CRIC coordinate with various

---

12. Consejo Regional Indígena del Cauca (CRIC), *Nuestras Luchas de Ayer y de Hoy*, CRIC Booklet No. 1 (Popayán: CRIC, 1983), 24.

entities, including the traditional or higher authorities, the individual cabildos and associations of cabildos, and at the national level with the National Indigenous Organization of Colombia (ONIC).

The basic unit of government is the cabildos, who count on constitutional recognition as a traditional authority. The cabildo is actually inherited from the colonial period and "has been reformulated and assumed as its own organization, with collectively appointed authorities."[13] The cabildo, a kind of council, is the highest authority in a given reservation among the communities that elect it and the main way in which they exercise their autonomy.

The councils promote numerous projects and initiatives including community work or mingas, economic organizations independent of the State, traditional medicine, education, and sovereign justice. Since the colonial era, the governor has been the highest administrative figure, followed by mayors, the prosecutor, and treasurer, who make up the board of directors of the council, while the sheriffs represent each village or community, ranging between twenty and sixty members depending on the size of the reservation.

In principle, the positions are unpaid because they are considered a service to the community, although some governors and board members receive salaries. There are four objectives guiding the councils of the CRIC: unity, land, culture, and autonomy. All the councils have an Indigenous Guard, which is considered a key piece for the existence of their own power. Since culture is an inescapable starting point, they propose to concretize "Indigenous self-management and autonomy," in the conviction that it is not enough for the Constitution of the Colombian State to recognize the existence of Indigenous peoples, the goals of these councils are

---

13.   Eduardo Sandoval, *La Guardia Indígena Nasa y el Arte de La Resistencia Pacífica* (Colombia: Ediciones Colección Étnica—Diálogos Interculturales–Fundación HEMERA, 2008), 39.

not carried out through advocacy but "are achieved through political struggle and the struggle for land in alliance with the other exploited and oppressed sectors of the country."[14]

In 1994, probably the most important association of Indigenous councils in Cauca emerged: Asociación de Cabildos Indígenas del Norte del Cauca, or ACIN (Association of Indigenous Councils of Northern Cauca). ACIN has developed important programs in health, education, economy, community development, communication, and the law. In 2005, the ACIN convened the Black and mestizo peasant communities of the region to an interethnic meeting, which led to the creation of "an autonomous interethnic region" in the municipalities of northern Cauca. Among the standout productive projects of this association are a fish station, a dairy processor, and a fruit juice plant.[15]

ACIN's educational development has been remarkable; thousands of children take courses across 156 schools, and older students attend an Indigenous center of higher education. CECIDIC (Center for Education, Training, and Research for the Integral Development of the Community) is dedicated to teaching their own history and cultural practices, economics, and agribusiness. It has established technical training schools in agroecology, arts and crafts, and political and pedagogical training, as well as a communications school.

The center opened in 1990 when the communities of the Toribío region recovered a territory of around ninety-six hectares, tilled the land, and planted and erected fences at night to avoid repression. Later on, they handed over the tenure to the council "to materialize community dreams and hopes."[16] Hundreds of commu-

---

14. Sandoval, *La Guardia Indígena Nasa*, 43.

15. Anders Rudqvist and Roland Anrup, "Resistencia Comunitaria en Colombia. Los Cabildos Caucanos y Su Guardia Indígena," *Papel Político* 18, no. 2 (2013): 533.

16. Diego Fernando Yatacué Ortega, "CECIDIC: Del Enfoque Pedagógico Comunitario, Hacia el Camino del Sentir, Pensar y Vivir con Corazón

nity members were involved in the work to erect the first buildings, install a productive farm, arts and crafts spaces, and administrative areas.

CECIDIC has a community mandate that consists of supporting the Nasa people from the "pedagogy of feeling, thinking, and acting from the heart" so that the new generations are shaped by their own culture, customs, language—on their own territories.[17] Its main curricula is grounded in several key elements: strengthening the Indigenous Educational System through the revitalization of community pedagogy; strengthening the Nasa language (Nasayuwe); community accompaniment to strengthen family and collective autonomy; community research and education; and training for a dignified life in the territory.

One of the organizations that is strengthened in this process of recovering ancestry, community pedagogy, and "the practice of Nasa spirituality," considered "a deeply revolutionary act,"[18] is the Indigenous Guard itself, understood as one of the nuclei of the Nasa people, their identity, and their guide to other futures through the care of the territory.

Challenges of Creating Alternatives from Within

While inward or closed off collective practices present various benefits for communities, various challenges still persist. Although surpluses fill the needs of the reservation through an agreement

Nasa, Plan de Vida 'Proyecto Nasa', Territorio de Toribío–Cauca" (Bachelor's Thesis, Universidad de Antioquia, 2019), 78.

17. Diego Yatacué, "El CECIDIC: Veinte Años Tejiendo Sueños y Esperanzas en la Comunidad Nasa," Grupo Semillas website, December 22, 2016, https://semillas.org.co/es/revista/el-cecidic-veinte-aos-tejiendo-sueos-y-esperanzas-en-la-comunidad-nasa.

18. Yatacué, "CECIDIC," 89.

between the cabildo authorities and communities, it does not mean that there are no inequalities or capitalist social relations within the enterprises.

The former director of CECIDIC, Diego Yatacué, eloquently explains this challenge while discussing the "new problems" facing the Nasa community: "Freedom and rights were given to the people, but they were not educated at home, so we have a high social and family degradation, young people without parental guidance who are exposed to modern life and consumerism; an eagerness to obtain money whatever its origin, whether from illicit crops, businesses measured by profitability (increase in consumption of agro-toxins), the promotion of tourism that has not had enough analysis of its challenges; illegal but legal mining in Indigenous territories."[19]

Dependence on state resources for the operation of the Indigenous councils themselves, as well as the health and education system, and benefit programs such as Families in Action, is difficult to break from.[20] In short, there is false autonomy of families and individuals who, because they have enough money to buy what they need, think that they have managed to overcome poverty and need, and see communitarian, Indigenous authority and even that of the State as obstacles—the real enemies.

Something similar is happening with respect to the election of authorities in some reservations. For several years, at least in northern Cauca, the traditional electoral practice of electing governors and other authorities from lists that follow propaganda campaigns, similar to that used to elect state representatives, has been abandoned. Instead, people are being chosen based upon their "spiritual" criteria. Each village proposes the person it considers most suitable,

19.   Yatacué, "CECIDIC," 80.
20.   Families in Action, or Familias en Acción, is a state benefits program for those with dependents.

according to the principles of the Nasa worldview, and in an assembly of the cabildo, the elders elect the six or seven most suitable people to occupy positions.[21]

The Indigenous Guard as an Engine for Communal Democracy

When the peoples of Cauca, and in particular the Nasa, refer to the Indigenous Guard, they go back to a five-hundred-year history of resistance. "The Indigenous Guard is a tradition of resistance that can be seen as far back as the year 1500," explains Alfredo Muelas, who was a coordinator of the Guard between 1999 and 2004.[22] Others consider the Guard "the legitimate daughter of time and history . . . heiress of the secular Nasa struggles."[23] In any case, it is an ancestral organism of its own, "an instrument of unity, resistance, and ethnic and territorial autonomy."[24]

History reveals how important the memory of resistance and struggles were in the construction of the new Indigenous Guard that emerged at the beginning of the twentieth century. It was formed in the face of the permanent aggression suffered by the communities at the hands of the army, paramilitaries, and the guerrillas, all within the framework of the extensive Colombian armed conflict.

Some authors identify up to five key moments that inform the current Indigenous Guard. The first was recorded around 1500 by La Gaitana, chieftain of the Tierradentro region, who led thousands of Indigenous warriors against the Spaniards between 1539 and 1540. The second moment was carried out in 1700 by Juan Tama, cacique

---

21. Exchange with Berta Camprubí, December 9, 2020.
22. Sandoval, *La Guardia Indígena Nasa*, 47.
23. Nelson Murillo Sepulveda, "La Guardia Indígena Nasa: Formas de Defensa de La Vida y La Madre Tierra En Toribío–Cauca" (Master's Thesis, Universidad Santo Tomás, Bogotá, 2015), 70.
24. Murillo, "La Guardia Indígena Nasa," 70.

of Vitoncó between 1682 and 1718, whose struggle left behind seventy-one colonial titles by which the Spanish crown legally recognized as Indigenous territories.[25] The third moment was the struggle of Manuel Quintín Lame at the beginning of the twentieth century. He mobilized thousands of Indigenous people from various departments for the recovery of lost lands. This uprising fought to limit the expansion of haciendas by fighting landowners, and led to his persecution and his 108 total imprisonments, later considered "the first Indigenous thinker" of Colombia.[26] Quintín Lame's work became a school of thought, his writings circulated in workshops, assemblies, and reading circles that still exist today, and he played a decisive role in the creation of the main Nasa organizations, especially in the CRIC and the Indigenous Guard.[27]

The fourth moment is precisely the formation of the CRIC, in 1971, which incorporates the three processes previously mentioned. CRIC was born at a time of generalized repression and great struggle for poor peasants in the Asociación Nacional de Usuarios Campesinos (ANUC, National Association of Peasant Smallholders), within which the Indigenous people became aware of the difference in their identity, history, and culture. The seven points of the CRIC program echo the objectives of Quintín Lame, who died in 1967 when the Indigenous movement was struggling against *terraje*, a form of serfdom that landholders advanced following the end official end of slavery in Colombia in 1851.[28] Some historians of the movement maintain that "the current Indigenous

25. Sandoval, *La Guardia Indígena Nasa*, 48.
26. Renán Vega, Gente Muy Rebelde 2: Indígenas, Campesinos y Protestas Agrarias (Bogotá: Pensamiento Crítico, 2002), 101.
27. Manuel Quintín Lame, "Los Pensamientos Del Indio Que Se Educó Dentro de las Selvas Colombianas," *Revista Colombiana de Educación* 48 (June 2005).
28. Lorenzo Muelas Hurtado, "La Fuerza de La Gente: Juntando Recuerdos Sobre la Terrajería en Guambía-Colombia," *Maguaré* (2005).

Guard is that of the past but in the present," although "it has under-gone changes adapting to political, social, economic, and religious conditions in specific times."[29]

The fifth moment occurred in the 1980s, with the formation of the Quintín Lame Armed Movement (MAQL). This armed guer-rilla organization, which is made up of Indigenous people, "did not seek to seize power but ensured the security of Indigenous commu-nities against the assassinations paid for by the landowners—called 'birds'—and against the armed entities of the state that threatened communities."[30] This guerrilla group was never autonomous, but the recruitment and education of the combatants was intimately linked to the cabildos, to the point that it can be said that "the Quintín Lame was another arm of the Indigenous Guard, it was the armed defense of the territory."[31]

When the combatants ultimately decided to name the group Quintín Lame, they had also discussed calling it Juan Tama or Cacica Gaitana, which reveals the importance of history on the struggle of the communities. At that time Quintín was unknown in the communities and also among most of the leaders, but the MAQL played a decisive role in the "dissemination of Lamista thinking" that has occurred mainly orally.[32] Indeed, those who reis-sued Lame's work were members of the MAQL, which shows that the Indigenous Guard (both current and previous) play a decisive role not only in community care but also in community education.

The current Indigenous Guard emerged toward the end of the twentieth century and appeared "visibly in Jambaló in 2000, with the dismantling of laboratories to process cocaine," and with

29. Sandoval, *La Guardia Indígena Nasa*, 50.
30. Joanne Rappaport, "Manuel Quintín Lame Hoy," in *Los Pensamientos del Indio Que Se Educó Dentro de Las Selvas Colombianas*, ed. Cristóbal Gnecco (Popayán: Universidad del Cauca, 2004), 73.
31. Sandoval, *La Guardia Indígena Nasa*, 51.
32. Rappaport, "Manuel Quintín Lame Hoy," 87.

the establishment of a night watch in order to prevent a massacre since they were unarmed and sought to avoid confrontations with paramilitaries, guerrillas, and the army.[33] The Guard is made up of thousands of young people, children, women, and adults, chosen by their communities to serve in tasks of "surveillance, control, warning, protection, and defense of our land in coordination with traditional authorities and the community."[34]

The structure of the Guard is very simple and is ordered from top to bottom: each village or community elects ten Guards and a coordinator through assembly; then a coordinator is elected by ballot and another for the entire region, always in agreement with the governors of the councils. The Guards are elected for two or three years, as agreed on by the councils. In 2010 in northern Cauca there were thirty-five hundred Guards, but their number varies according to the conflicts that exist, the strength of the cabildo, and the communities.

I interviewed Luis Alberto Mensa in 2008, when he was coordinator of all the Guards of the region: "Training is our most important aspect and we do it through workshops where human rights and our law, the original law, are discussed. We prioritize political training over physical exercises."[35] The workshops are mandatory and last several days. They involve community leaders who relate the history and usos y costumbres of the Nasa people. Then each coordinator replicates the same workshops on their own properties. "We are the trainers in the organization, we are the protection of the community and defense of life without getting involved in war," Mensa continues. The coordinator of the

33.   Sandoval, *La Guardia Indígena Nasa,* 53.
34.   CRIC, "Qué es la Guardia Indígena y Porqué es Tan Importante Para la Defensa Territorial?" Servindi website, February 14, 2015, https://www .servindi.org/actualidad/123279.
35.   Raúl Zibechi, "Colombia: Autoprotección Indígena."

Huellas Guard, Manuel Ul, maintains that the political education they provide "contributes to preventing young people from joining armed groups."

As participation in the Indigenous Guard is voluntary, the neighbors of the village and the authorities of the cabildo collaborate in the maintenance of the family garden and sometimes call for mingas to clear, sow, or harvest it. The Guards are trained intensely on the Nasa worldview that rejects violence, they practice forms of defense through warnings, and stand between the armed militias in large groups to dissuade them from attacking the community. The Guard are summoned in their native language on local radio stations and by cell phones. In just four hours they can gather hundreds of Guards from across the reservation.

The central aspect of the Indigenous Guard is that it "represents and is a real and symbolic depository of otherness."[36] Here, an alterity is reflected in a history that is different from that of Afro-Colombians, mestizos, and white Creoles; one that is seen in its own worldview, in the Nasa identity and culture, in the form of relating with Mother Earth. It is one that is recognized in a variety of ceremonies that aims to revive history as a living memory and to seek harmony between people, and between them and the natural environment. Otherness is also political. "Nasa alterity does not seek the seizure of political power, nor armed confrontation against its aggressors. On the contrary, it demands autonomy and respect for its people and its culture within the limits of the state, without transcending its territories, its being, and its thinking."[37]

Nasa otherness explains the need for autonomy but from it they also deduce their rejection of war and violence. Don Pedro has lived in Caloto for over sixty years. He served his people as

---

36. Sandoval, *La Guardia Indígena Nasa*, 53.
37. Sandoval, *La Guardia Indígena Nasa*, 56.

governor of the Cabildo de Huellas, mayor, and secretary, is part of the process of liberation of Mother Earth, and belongs to the first generation of Nasa fighters who gave life to the CRIC. In his village he is considered an elder, and I was able to interview him during the pandemic on this topic:

> Among us there was no war but balance and harmony, but the arrival of the settlers was the beginning of a war for territory. The liberation of Mother Earth is the way to reconstruct our history as we rebuild our territory. We do not want war, but we have to defend ourselves. For us, defending ourselves is recovering land and reconstructing our historical memory is our way of confronting this neoliberal policy of destruction. Through education, the state has created a strategy to subdue us in order for us to lose our culture. The paramilitaries kill us [physically] and they kill us ideologically and politically with education. The goal is to continue to survive; the guard is responsible for protecting the community. But sometimes you have to fight and go on the offensive.[38]

By "offensive" he means strikes, mingas, and mobilizations so that the State complies with the agreements on health, land delivery, and education. One of the slogans of the CRIC reads: "Count on us for peace, never for war."

Miguel, who is forty-four, lives in the López adentro reservation, formed in the 1970s with almost three thousand community members, it shares its territory with the Afro-descendant population of the region. "Not taking up the gun is not a symptom of weakness but a different culture and worldview than the oppressor." If culture

---

38. Exchange with Don Pedro and Miguel, September 25, 2020. For security reasons, both preferred to adopt fictitious names.

and worldview are different from hegemonic ones, they cannot act in the same way as militants, paramilitaries, and revolutionary movements. "We talk about building, jointly, but the rebels want to build through the force of arms and talk about taking power, while we talk about managing well, about our simple life. That war is not ours. They want to impose it on us and involve our young people."

The Indigenous Guard defends autonomy and self-government, the Nasa Project or "life plan" and has been defined as "a minga in resistance for protection and territorial control with humanitarian and solidarity accompaniment for the defense of life."[39] Rooted in cultural traditions and in the long history of its people, it defends life, protects the people, and establishes collective care based on its own right. In demonstrations it is about protection; in assemblies and rituals it is accompaniment and vigilance; in serious crises such as the kidnappings of leaders or assassinations, it enacts huge mobilizations to rescue or deter violence, wielding its batons of command and its ceremonial scarves. In critical moments they take up the Nasa creed, *todos somos guardia* (we are all Guards), because it is a community organized and mobilized in collective self-defense, motivated by its own mystique cultivated in rituals.

But that is just the outside or visible part. What is less seen are the tasks of the Guard toward the interior of the Indigenous world. On the one hand, the Guard does not rule alone, it obeys the councils, the communities, and the elders and mayors who are the symbolic and ethical authorities. In this sense, there is no separation between the Guards and community, as there is between police and society. On the other hand, their training is particularly intense among young people, often tempted by guerrillas and especially drug traffickers to join their ranks. According to Eduardo Sandoval's study, there are three dimensions of the action of armed

---

39. Sandoval, *La Guardia Indígena Nasa*, 61.

groups taken against the Indigenous world: they incorporate young people into their ranks in order to divide communities; they later seek to pull apart the Indigenous movement and, ultimately, seek to annihilate it.[40]

Training has several dimensions in the Nasa communities. One aspect is the training across special schools, including the Escuela de Derecho Propio, the Escuela de Medicina Tradicional, and several other institutions. Another prominent part of training is the *tulpa* (stove) where they are in dialogue with and listening to the elderly, as well as their participation in the rituals of harmonization. The Guard thus plays a role of internal regulation to maintain harmony, because it is a cohesive force, as Sandoval said in his research. Every six months, or once a year, they participate in rituals where the ceremonial cane and Guards are harmonized. These are led by traditional doctors (*thé walas*) and include bathing in the rivers and ceremonies that strengthen solidarity and reciprocity. These rituals are "expressions of Nasa resistance," because these are people facing very violent situations that often put their lives at risk.[41]

Indigenous Guard, Popular Revolt, and Horizons of Change

The two-month long general strike in 2021 began at 5:30 a.m. on April 28 in Cali. It was initiated with the demolition of the statue of the city's founder, the conqueror Sebastián de Belalcázar by a group of Misak Indigenous people. Fifty-eight authorities from three Misak communities prosecuted the conquistador for "genocide, land grabbing, and the rape of women in the period of the Spanish conquest."[42] Every revolt took place with the presence of thousands

---

40. Sandoval, *La Guardia Indígena Nasa*, 91.
41. Sandoval, *La Guardia Indígena Nasa*, 75.
42. Juan Echeverri, "ESPECIAL: Cali, sucursal de la resistencia," *Periferia*,

of Indigenous Guard at various "points of resistance" across Cali in a spectacular display of solidarity and commitment to urban youth.[43]

In one of its most notable interventions, the Guard managed to arrest one of the armed civilians who shot at protesters in Cali. Giovannny Yule, a coordinator for the Indigenous Guard, said the protesters called the Guard because they were being attacked by armed men. "The Guard must be peaceful, and without weapons, because only the organizational and collective exercise of the community is capable of neutralizing anyone who is armed," he told the media while calling on urban dwellers to "create their own community guards" to act collectively to neutralize those who threaten life.[44]

This long Colombian revolt, focused on the big cities, is an opportunity for the most dynamic sectors of the Indigenous movement. Among them and in a prominent place is the Indigenous Guard, as they revitalize the movement to limit the main "ambiguities" that anchor the peoples to the system and enhance the transformative aspects that call it into question.

At the end of October 2020, the Indigenous, Black, and Peasant

June 8, 2021, https://periferiaprensa.com/cali-sucursal-de-la-resistencia.

43. In Cali, twenty-five "points of resistance" were formed. These were collective spaces of coexistence in popular or central neighborhoods in which young people and those of all ages participated, and were defended by the "first lines," made up of young people of both sexes. There were also "front lines" in several cities of the country constituted of mothers to protect their children, religious figures, and even retired military. See Lluis Muñoz Pandiella, "Colombia: En el Barrio de Puerto Resistencia, Hasta los Predicadores Marchan, *France 24*, May 7, 2021, https://www.france24.com/es/am%C3%A9rica-latina/20210507-protestas-colombia-cali-puerto-resistencia-guardia-indigena-pueblo-nasa.

44. "Video: Minga Indígena Capturó a Hombre Que Estaría Implicado en Tiroteo Contra Manifestantes en Cali," video, *Infobae*, May 8, 2021, https://www.infobae.com/america/colombia/2021/05/08/video-minga-indigena-capturo-a-hombre-que-estaria-implicado-en-tiroteo-contra-manifestantes-en-cali.

National minga was held. It started in the Southwest, in Cauca, and continued onto Cali, touring several cities and towns before arriving in the capital, Bogotá, eight days later. Throughout its journey, the minga spoke with populations who share similar painful struggles—not very hard to find in a country that has experienced widespread narco-military-paramilitary violence and the killing of hundreds of social leaders.

Eight thousand native, Black, and peasant peoples participated in the minga to Bogotá, escorted by the Indigenous Guard, with the strong prominence of women and young people. The minga was received and accompanied by thousands of people who had been fighting against the repression of various militarized entities. According to the various sources, there are between forty- and sixty-thousand self-defense peoples' Guards across the country's 115 Indigenous communities. Each pueblo counts on its own sovereign territories: Black *palenques* and peasant reserve areas join the Indigenous reservations, forming a multicolored tapestry of struggles of resistance and dignity.

In this ongoing growth, we can again distinguish between two dimensions: the outward and inward. Sketching what is happening in both is a kind of provisional conclusion of this chapter.

Outward there is a horizontal expansion of the Guards. If at the beginning of the millennium they could be counted in the hundreds, during the pandemic it was only the CRIC that was able to organize in this way, mobilizing seven thousand Guards to control the entry and exit points of the reservations.

This remarkable growth was consolidated during the months of the 2021 revolt. But the most notable expansion is the one that has occurred in recent years in Black and peasant communities. In 1993, the Black Communities Process was created in Palenque, Alto Cauca, and today includes 140 grassroots organizations and community councils that intend to defend "their own political-organizational autonomy."[45] In 2009 the first Maroon Guard was created in Palenque and in 2013 the first National Congress of Black Communities was held, which made the Guard official. The Peasant Guards, which were formalized in the 2010s, are on the other hand inspired by the antecedent of the civic guards of 1974 within the framework of the ANUC. As of 2018, interethnic and intercultural meetings of Guards are held every year.[46]

As the aforementioned work points out, "the history of each guard and their level of care are different, as it is also clear that many of the problems they face are shared."[47] The Peasant Guards, for example, are actually community networks set up to defend the territory without the permanence or organizational structure of their Indigenous and Maroon peers. However, the existence of a relationship between these various guards, allows us to ensure that the rich Nasa experience is being sown not only among the other native peoples of Colombia, but also in the cities, something that years ago seemed impossible.

Inwardly, the work of the Indigenous Guard can be indirectly felt through the strengthening of their own governments and the various initiatives that have agglomerated during the 2021 revolt: the First Meeting of Young People of the First Line in Huila at the beginning of July, the III Regional Meeting of Education within the framework of the norms of the Sistema Educativo Indígena Propio (SEIP) at the end of June in that year, the meeting to strengthen the pedagogical strategies of self-education the first week of July

45. Proceso de Comunidades Negras-PCN (2021) "¡Somos Proceso de Comunidades Negrasen Colombia!," https://renacientes.net/quienes-somos (accessed 10/1/2023).

46. Axel Rojas Martinez and Vanessa Useche, *Guardias Indigenas, Afrodescendientes y Campesinas* (Popayán: Universidad del Cauca, 2019), https://www.academia.edu/43747197/Guardias_indigenas_afro descendientes_y_campesinas.

47. Rojas and Useche, *Guardias Indigenas*, 34.

in Tierradentro, the XVI Assembly of Indigenous Women that shows the growing participation of women at all levels of the Nasa Çxhâçxha Association organization.[48]

I want to emphasize that revolt is the engine of change in Colombia and that the Indigenous Guard was not content with just defending the reservations but went down to Cali, got involved with the young people in struggle, and thus soaked up the environment that reigns in the cities. Between five and seven thousand Nasa Indigenous peoples, organized as guards, participated directly in the revolt, especially the young. They did not go to direct or give orders, but to accompany the mobilizations.[49]

These ventures only strengthen the activist spirit of the Guard. Proof of this can be found in the proposed debates by the Communication Fabric of the ACIN, another of the most advanced nodes of the movement. In the middle of the revolt, they published a well-circulated text, titled: "No Se Triunfa Si No Se Piensa la Autonomía por Fuera del Estado y Si Hay Autonomía con Patriarcado" (We cannot succeed if we do not think about autonomy beyond the State and if patriarchy remains).[50]

During the celebrations of the fiftieth anniversary of the CRIC, held weeks before the revolt, many self-critical voices were heard, such as those of Gentil Guejia, a Nasa member from the Tierradentro region who works in education from the *tulpa*: "We value the strength of the CRIC, the ability to convene, but we also

48. CRIC, "60 años de Cárcel."
49. Lina Vargas, "La Guardia Indígena Protege a los Manifestantes en Cali," *Gatopardo*, May 27, 2021, https://gatopardo.com/noticias-actuales/la-guardia-indigena-protege-a-los-manifestantes-en-cali.
50. Consejo Regional Indígena Del Cauca (CRIC), "'No Se Triunfa Si No Se Piensa la Autonomía por Fuera del Estado y Si Hay Autonomía con Patriarcado," CRIC website, May 26, 2021, https://www.cric-colombia.org/portal/no-se-triunfa-si-no-se-piensa-la-autonomia-por-fuera-del-estado-y-si-hay-autonomia-con-patriarcado.

question the way in which it has been institutionalized, for example, with education, there we are still on a borrowed path."[51]

It is on this path that we can find the reflection of Aida Quilcué, one of the most respected voices in the Nasa world: "Let's check ourselves inward. Let's do what you, the community, have called the minga inward, go toward the life that identifies us from the roots, that is part of the resistance." In her opinion, this is the way to deepen the otherness of the Indigenous world, in order to contain and overcome the "five-hundred-year political, cultural, and spiritual invasion."[52]

51. Berta Camprubí, "El CRIC Colombiano Cumple Medio Siglo de Lucha Indígena," *El Salto*, March 7, 2021, https://www.elsaltodiario.com/pueblos-originarios/-el-cric-colombiano-cumple-medio-siglo-de-lucha-indigena.
52. Camprubí, "El CRIC Colombiano."

Imaginary Dialogues with Öcalan
Updating Critical Thinking

The generations that entered political life in the 1960s had the privilege of witnessing a world in turmoil, with permanent and unpredictable changes that took place under abrupt crises and extraordinary turns. In the words of historian Eric Hobsbawm, we lived in interesting times. We lived in the times of the Cuban revolution (1959), of valiant and inspiring Algerian people's resistance against the French occupying forces (1954–1962), of the heroic resistance of the Vietnamese people who taught the world that even the greatest military power in history could be defeated.

Beyond wars, spectacular events and new kinds of power during those years came to redefine an era: Black mobilization in the United States against racial segregation; the movement led by the Black Panther Party, the most radical and consistent episode of those turbulent years. The Cultural Revolution in China seemed like a fresh wind against the bureaucracies that, in the name of socialism, had clung to power throughout Eastern Europe and the Soviet Union, and were beginning to surface in Mao's land. Its most valuable lesson being that only by mobilizing the people could limits be placed on a bureaucracy that became a new ruling class. The young people of Prague, saddling the Warsaw Pact tanks in the streets, spoke in the same direction as the young Chinese radicals who waved Mao's red book.

A whole generation of rebels was born into political life in the midst of this set of movements that, through the vantage point of time, left nothing in place. A defining characteristic of the movements of the 1960s, and of the world revolution of 1968, is that after beginning on the periphery of the world-system their resounding proclamations were made in the centers of the world-system. The events in Paris in May 1968, as well as the large student demonstrations on university campuses of the United States, would not have been possible without Algeria or Vietnam, for example, and neither without the massacre of the Plaza de Tlatelolco, on October 2, 1968, in Mexico.

This is important because history teaches us that the most profound movements always begin in the peripheries, and then move to the center, although Eurocentric culture tends to make visible only the latter. Subcomandante Insurgente Marcos (now Galeano) said it very clearly: "The great transformations do not begin at the top, nor with monumental and epic events but with movements that are small in their form and that appear irrelevant to the politician and the analysts from above."[1] Zapatismo considers that the changes in history do not come from "full squares or indignant crowds," but from collectives that organize and coordinate "below and to the left and build another politics."[2]

It seems to me of the utmost importance because long before we knew about the current movement in Kurdistan, there were small changes that had not been noticed by the vast majority of those of us who consider ourselves anticapitalists, and we only take

---

1.   Subcomandante Insurgente Marcos, "Pensar el Blanco," First International Colloquium In Memory of Andrés Aubry, San Cristóbal de las Casas, Mexico, December 13, 2007, http://enlacezapatista.ezln.org .mx/2007/12/13/conferencia-del-dia-13-de-diciembre-a-las-900-am.
2.   Marcos, "Pensar el Blanco."

them into account when they appear in the mainstream media. In this case, we only noticed it in Latin America when in the mid-2010s self-governance was consolidated in Rojava and the media picked up this new reality. It is evident that we still need a lot of inner and collective work to continue decolonizing and de-patriarchalizing our critical thinking.

We must not forget that in the 1960s, Marxism-Leninism was common sense, as were ideologies with other surnames ranging from Stalinism to Maoism and Trotskyism. Although I consider myself to have a sharp memory, I cannot recall any of my comrades criticizing Marx's thought, although I must admit that some had been brought up in the basic religious communities that at the beginning of the 1970s already existed in the Río de la Plata in my home country of Uruguay.

The comrade who presided over the first political meeting I ever attended, on a sunny autumn Saturday at the Faculty of Architecture in Montevideo, placed the *Communist Manifesto* in front of our small group of pre-militants. Although the half dozen who participated in that initial event barely knew each other from secondary school, no one was surprised when the comrade said: "I must assume that we are all socialists."

It was the common sense of the time. And not the only one, by the way. "To be like Che," the phrase that said it all, was much more than respect for the revolutionary icon of the moment, who had fallen a year earlier in combat. It was a promise of life, given, if necessary, for the revolution that would bring happiness and well-being to the world. We repeated "being like Che" as a mantra in the face of any difficulty, and even out of habit. So ingrained was the feeling of fighting with arms in hand against the enemy that we never questioned it.

We made an imaginary game of chanting: "We shouted for Cuba and against imperialism. Do you?"

I imagine that in Turkey they would have other phrases/obsessions to lift spirits, disperse fears, and strengthen the fighting spirit. I would like to know them, although I must assume that they would relate to the history of the Kurdish people, to the infinity of heroes and heroines that that distant land has given.

I imagine that the slogans would be against the Turkish regime, with that succession of coups d'état that the military gave with strange punctuality: 1960, 1971, 1980. . . I am surprised by the coincidences. In our South America, if not in all of Latin America, there were coups d'état, mass imprisonments and torture, disappearances, and paramilitary groups, different and in some ways similar to those of the Bozkurtlar (Grey Wolves) that murdered leftist militants in Turkey.

There must also be a few differences that at some point I would like to know. I mean the long stories, what it feels like to be part of a people without a state, something that the political currents to which we belonged in the 1970s had not theorized because common sense told us that a revolution was neither possible nor desirable if it was not focused on the State (to take it or annihilate it).

What impresses me most about Öcalan's thinking is his ability to change while being faithful to the objectives.

Let me explain.

Even the wise men of my/our generation have shown how difficult it is to move from what we have learned, how stubborn the ideas that we internalize in our youth are. Fernand Braudel, whom Öcalan quotes on several occasions, rightly stated once that "mental frameworks are also long-term prisons." Overcoming these theoretical frameworks requires a lot of intellectual courage and a lot of honesty, because it is as much about looking in the mirror and recognizing the limitations of our thinking and our movements.

I have the highest esteem for Abdullah Öcalan's trajectory. Because he was not satisfied with repeating over and over again

what he had learned. Because he had the courage to make a turn—
or several—when things were no longer working according to
the old patterns of Marxism-Leninism, remaining shipwrecked in
orthodoxy. For wasn't Lenin heterodoxic about Marx? As was Mao's
about Stalin? Overcoming orthodoxy is not merely a theoretical
question, but an ethical one, attached to truth and to the people.

It is not a theoretical question because it does not make the
slightest sense to cling to a set of ideas acquired in a given context
and repeat them when that context has changed. For revolutionaries, unlike academics, ideas are not an end in themselves, we do
not defend certain ideas to give us importance or to be recognized
as intellectuals. Ideas are only means. The only end is the people,
the common people, those from below, or whatever we want to
call the real people to whom we have committed ourselves and
struggled.

When the Zapatistas were a few dozen fighters and took their
first village, they addressed its inhabitants in a dialogue that shows
how theories can be an obstacle to working with the people: "What
were you telling them?" a journalist asked Subcomandante Marcos.
"Well, the absurdities that we had learned, that imperialism, the
social crisis, the correlation of forces and the conjuncture, things
that nobody understood, of course, and neither did they. They were
very honest. You'd ask them, 'Did you understand?' and they'd say,
'No.' You had to adapt," says Marcos.[3]

They told him that his words were "very harsh," and so
they decided to talk about the history of Mexico but making an
Indigenist history, focused on people like them. It was the combatants of Indigenous origin who began to explain the history of the
country. They appropriated their own history, because they acted

---

3.   Subcomandante Insurgente Marcos, "Entrevista con Carmen Castillo,"
     Contrahistorias 20 (October 1994), 63.

as translators while, says Marcos, "we became spectators." The next step was to learn to listen, because not only did they speak in other ways but "their references, their cultural framework, were different." The result was that a hybrid was born, the product of a crash in which "fortunately, I think, we lost."

What was defeated in this meeting was a patriarchal and Eurocentric orthodoxy. It is a necessary defeat and is the product of rootedness in the people.

Circling back to Öcalan, I want to highlight the importance of having elevated the role of women, of recognizing the central place the patriarchy holds as a mode of domination closely linked to capitalism and colonialism. It is a profound change within critical thinking, because neither in the 1960s nor in the 1970s did we have that view of the world as women were marginalized. And neither did they occupy it in Marxism or Leninism, or even in other later strands. As far as I know, the Kurdish revolutionary movement is the one that is working on the women's issue in greater depth, where the issue of women's oppression runs through the whole movement, in all of its facets and activities.

After these important ethical-political considerations, I would like to address some of Öcalan's ideas that we come to know through his works from the prison of Imrali.[4]

It is very difficult to synthesize his ideas and his contributions to the revolutionary movements of the world given the enormous diversity of topics that he addresses as well as the very broad view of his analysis. But it is difficult, above all, because he has taken both the rejection of capitalist civilization and the shortcut that real socialism took as his starting point.

This is one of the keys to the profound radicality of Öcalan's

4. Long considered the "Guantanamo Bay of Europe," Imrali is a high security prison on an island in the Sea of Marmara, where Öcalan has spent most of his imprisonment as the sole inmate there.

thought. He believes that the civilizational crisis cannot be overcome either with the restoration of fascism or with actually existing socialism. Contrary to what most of the left thinks, it is not a question of "returning" to statist socialism, improved by the extirpation of its "deviations" but something much deeper that happens to create something theoretically and politically new. Needless to say, this rootedness bothers both classical intellectuals and orthodox militants.

What is striking about Öcalan's work in prison, however, is the coherence of his thought across all his texts. It considers the emancipation of women, the protection of nature, and the control of the harmful effects of technology to be paramount. These are the main conclusions of his extensive reconstruction of the history of civilizations, from his Mesopotamian gaze looking out from the banks of the Euphrates and the Tigris.

The prominent role that Öcalan attributes to ethics in the construction of a new world is a neuralgic point that can go hand in hand with other issues that are left aside in the socialist camp: the importance of individuality (which is not synonymous with individualism), since we aspire to a society of free individuals, the precondition for them to take responsibility for their actions, as well as the restoration of the role of civil society, which in Öcalan's language is defined as the "third domain."

From my point of view, inevitably focused on Latin America, Öcalan manages to advance on the Eurocentric theories of capitalist modernity, which is a greater merit that places him in a prominent place of critical and emancipatory thinking in this historical period. His work rejects the modern tabula rasa theory (which says the past must be annihilated)—which inspired various movements from the Jacobins to the Bolsheviks—and proposes to rescue that past as one of the resources the future society could use to build the long-awaited "democratic civilization."

I find resonance here with the concrete experience of the Indigenous movements of my continent. In particular, the work of reconstructing the history of Öcalan connects me with the phrase of an Ecuadorian Indigenous leader, a Kichwa lawyer who is in charge of Ecuarinari, one of the most important organizations in the country. "We walk in the footsteps of our ancestors," Carlos Pérez Guartambel told me in his village, surrounded by community members who resist mining and defend water and life.

Like the Latin American Indigenous movements, Öcalan's work manages to amalgamate the cultural traditions of the Middle East with a proposal of transformation for the entire Kurdish society. The place from which a discourse, analysis, and theory is issued and elaborated, must be located somewhere. This is true except for Eurocentric thought that has a vocation to turn one's own vision into universal truth. A history that starts from the peoples that inhabited Mesopotamia, can only enrich the history of all peoples, since their particularities add to the universal.

I believe that both Öcalan's thinking and what is happening in Rojava in recent years is in tune with what a good part of the Latin American social movements are doing. To a large extent, because both of us have been colonized by the West and our peoples had to withdraw into themselves to survive. Our respective regions needed to close themselves in their communities and their ancestral cultures, as "tombs" in which it was possible to re-create life.

At least three resonances can be found between these movements.

The first concerns the nation-state. Diverse peoples, such as the Mapuche of Chile and Argentina, the Nasa of southern Colombia, the Aymara of Bolivia, and the Indigenous people of the Amazon and the lowlands, do not identify with the states or seek to obtain positions in state institutions. The new Black/Afro-descendant movements in Colombia and Brazil are following similar processes, distancing themselves from the political theater of the nation-state.

It is not an ideological question. For most of them, nation-states are not part of their histories and experiences as peoples; they are understood as an imposition of colonialism and Creole elites. The Kurds of Rojava do not intend to build a State. Öcalan regards the nation-state as the form of power appropriate for "capitalist civilization." For Kurds who share his ideas, the anti-state struggle is even more important than the class struggle, which is considered heresy by the Latin American leftists still looking toward the nineteenth-century strategy. These leftists continue to regard the State as a shield to protect the workers.

In fact, the Kurdish leader holds a thesis very close to the Zapatista practice. The seizure of the State, writes Öcalan, perverts the most faithful revolutionary, to conclude with a reflection that sounds appropriate to remember the centenary of the Russian Revolution: "A hundred and fifty years of heroic struggle was overwhelmed by the gulf of power."[5]

The second resonance is in the economy. The Zapatistas often mock the "laws" of the economy and do not place that discipline at the center of their thinking, as seems evident in the collection of communiqués of the former Subcomandante Marcos. Öcalan, for his part, emphasizes that "capitalism is not economy but power."[6] Capitalists use the economy, but the core of the system is force, armed and unarmed, to confiscate the surpluses that society produces.

Zapatismo defines the current extractive model (monocultures, such as soybeans, open-pit mining, and mega infrastructure works) as a "Fourth World War" against the peoples, using force to delineate

5. Abdullah Öcalan, *Manifesto for a Democratic Civilization*, Vol. II, *Capitalism: The Age of Unmasked Gods and Naked Kings* (Porsgrunn, Norway: New Compass Press, 2017), 315.

6. Öcalan, *Manifesto*, Vol. II, 130.

societies. In both movements there is a clear criticism of economism. Öcalan recalls that "no economic rules underlay the colonial wars where the initial accumulation was extorted."[7] Indigenous and Black movements in Latin America, for their part, describe the nucleus of domination in this continent to be colonial power, or "coloniality of power," a term coined by Peruvian sociologist Aníbal Quijano.

Indeed, economism is a plague that contaminates critical movements, which goes hand in hand with evolutionism. A legion of leftists believe that the end of capitalism will be produced by the succession of more or less profound economic crises. Öcalan opposes this perspective and rejects the proposal of those who believe that capitalism was born "as a natural result of economic development."[8] Zapatistas and Kurds seem to agree with Walter Benjamin's thesis that progress is a destructive hurricane.

Contrary how those of us who have been trained in Marxthink, Öcalan argues that a good part of the analyses of economic specialists is merely mythological rations that lay the foundations of a new religion: "Political economy is the most fraudulent and predatory monument of fictive intelligence, developed to disguise the speculative character of capitalism."[9] He agrees here with Braudel that capitalism is the negation of the market by the price regulation of monopolies, which prevents the competition of producers. Carrying on with his contrarian position, he rejects that the triumph of capitalism has added anything revolutionary and, on this point, agrees with the analysis of Immanuel Wallerstein when he assures that capitalism has not been "progress" compared to other historical systems. That is why he maintains that what is truly revolutionary is not when the worker fights for his rights against the boss but that he "resists being a proletarian, who fights against unemployment as

7.   Öcalan, *Manifesto*, Vol. II, 66.
8.   Öcalan, *Manifesto*, Vol. II, 64.
9.   Öcalan, *Manifesto*, Vol. II, 73.

much as against the status of worker because that struggle would be more socially meaningful and ethical." In this way, his theory recovers the most radical and anticapitalist tradition of critical thought that has almost entirely been lost in our moment.

The third resonance I find in Öcalan's thought is with Latin American movements defending *good living/living well* comparably opposing capitalist productivism. The constitutions of Ecuador and Bolivia, approved in 2008 and 2009 respectively, emphasized that nature is a "subject bestowed with rights," when it had previously been considered an object simply from which to obtain wealth. Among these movements we find the idea that we are facing something much more profound than a crisis of capitalism: a civilizational crisis. The Kurdish movement maintains that capitalism leads to the crisis of modern Western capitalist civilization, an analysis that allows us to overcome the ideology of progress and development, integrates the various oppressions linked to patriarchy and racism, the environmental and the health crisis, and takes a deeper and broader look at the ongoing crises.

A civilization enters into crisis when it no longer has the resources (material and symbolic) to solve the problems it has created. That is why movements so distant—geographically and culturally—feel that humanity is on the threshold of a new world. I believe that Öcalan has gone much further than other militants of our generation in his criticism of Marxism, as well as of Marx. When he writes that Marx's work is tributary to "an 'enlightened' aberration" of a positivist and economistic stamp, and that it is about the vision of the world that he blames for the failure of a century and a half of struggles for freedom and for a democratic society, he is not only right in the analysis but also shows a free spirit that stops at nothing except for what he considers true.[10]

---

10.   Öcalan, *Manifesto*, Vol. II, 182.

In this way he recovers the rebellious spirit of Che Guevara when he vehemently argued with the Soviet bureaucracy without considering the consequences and what it meant for the relationship with the Soviet Union. Öcalan also brings to mind the rebellious and indomitable focus of Subcomandante Moisés when he analyzed the Zapatista construction of new worlds, and Subcomandante Marcos when he would not make the slightest concession to the reformist and progressive leftists.

In this way Abdullah Öcalan is holding a mirror up for the generation of the 1960s, so that we may look straight ahead at what we have lost in terms of a rebellious dignity to the altar of pragmatism and an accommodation to the dominant system. Defeat does not justify straying from the path, just as prison is not a reason to surrender. This dialogue with the thought and persistence of Öcalan, with his ability to make a turn without losing the way north even while imprisoned in Imrali, is an example for those of us who are still determined to change the world. Öcalan reminds us that it is impossible to change the world without first changing ourselves, because change, like movement itself, is singular and it is multiple, and we cannot afford to not be involved.

EZLN: Sowing Without Reaping

Zapatismo's longevity, profound changes over the years, and impressive capacity to transform itself time and again for the last four decades make it the most important movement for social change in the world today. I quite well understand that this statement may come off a bit too strongly for some, therefore, I think it warrants an explanation.

Four decades since their founding and three decades since the armed uprising, the EZLN have shown exceptional ethical and political coherence. During all these years they have kept their distance from Mexican governments and the world, asserting their autonomy and building a different, noncapitalist world while resisting the prevailing extractivist model.

During this time, they were able to set up a *new world* in their established territories. They set up health posts, clinics, and hospitals with an emphasis on prevention; set up hundreds of primary and secondary schools, as well as other training spaces; created an autonomous justice system functioning under its own criteria and separate from that of the State to which even non-Zapatista families have turned to.

They have set up an extensive network of productive spaces that has permitted them to become self-sufficient in organic food production while diversifying crops. They have created autonomous banks that support collective projects, artisan cooperatives, and many other food making cooperatives. They have also become well known for the production, distribution, and exportation of coffee. The Zapatistas have also developed artistic initiatives in music, dance, theater, and communication, among others.

Much of their structure relies on what are known as good governance boards (*juntas de buen gobierno*) and autonomous municipalities. The good governance boards are collective authorities made up equally of both men and women, whose membership rotates so that people learn to govern themselves based on the principle of "commanding by obeying."

All these initiatives were possible thanks to the collective work in their support bases and international and national solidarity, all the while never receiving any contributions from the State. The Zapatista world counts on almost no circulation of money while maintaining a strong anticapitalist structure.

For these reasons, Zapatismo has become an inescapable reference for the process of building autonomy in Latin America. Today, there are three autonomous governments in the northern Amazon of Peru, and several more in formation; there are twenty-six active autonomous protocols in place that demarcate land in the Brazilian Amazon across forty-eight territories where sixty-four Indigenous communities reside. In the southern Colombian region of Cauca, nine towns have formed their own authorities governing over their self-declared autonomous territories, grouped under the Regional Indigenous Council of Cauca (CRIC); there is also a broad process of recovering Mapuche lands where autonomous formations operate in southern Chile and Argentina.

Throughout the region, there are countless experiments of urban and rural autonomy, a few of them inspired by the uprising of January 1, 1994. However, referring to Zapatismo does not mean that everyone follows one of its postulates or its modes of construction. Autonomy has become a diverse and varied path, one replete with wide avenues through which different cultures and ways of doing things traverse. While they are still in the minority, they are no longer marginal.

※ ※ ※

Since October 22, 2023, the EZLN began issuing a series of communiqués in which it reported important changes to confront the new era of capitalist-modernity, what they refer to as the storm.[1] From now on, the good governance boards and autonomous municipalities, created two decades ago and a symbol of Zapatista self-government, have ceased to function. In place of the roughly thirty autonomous municipalities that were in existence, there will now be thousands of grassroots structures, local autonomous governments (LGAL), and hundreds of Zapatista autonomous government collectives (CGAZ).

I would like to breakdown four key elements I have identified in the succession of communiqués that show the depth of the Zapatista vision and project as this storm rages on.

The first is related to "long time," which looks ahead to seven generations, according to a passage in the communique titled "Dení," the name of a Mayan girl to be born in 120 years' time. The EZLN maintains that the "destruction comes faster. What we thought would happen in ten years is already here." They state that they have spent ten years preparing "for these days of pain and sorrow" and "self-critically reviewing what we do and what we don't do, what we say and don't say, what we think and look at."

---

1. The press releases can be found in chronological order at http://enlacezapatista.ezln.org.mx.

The recent decisions they have made keep this long horizon in mind. As they state, "we have to fight for someone we are not going to know," to make it possible for these new generations to be truly free and to take charge of the decisions they make, that is, the authors of their own freedom.

They bet on Dení to not only survive the ongoing storm but to go "through this and other storms that will come, it's about surviving the night, and reaching that morning, 120 years from now, where a girl begins to learn that being free is also being responsible for that freedom."

The EZLN observes that there will be wars, floods, droughts, and diseases ahead and therefore, "in the midst of collapse we have to look far ahead." We can debate the exact years this will take but what I think is most important is the centrality of the long horizon, and above all, what must be done in order to reach this period under better conditions. The Zapatistas add a decisively ethical issue, that of fighting for people who will never get to know one another, while noting that there will not be a "final victory," as we are accustomed to in revolutionary political cultures.

The second point is *self-criticism*, which is detailed in the communiqué entitled "Regarding Pyramids and Their uses and Customary Regimes."[2]

It should be noted that just as much as the left is obsessed with the time between elections, it also fails to critically review the decisions it makes.

In the "Regarding Pyramids and Their uses and Customary Regimes," the positive aspects of the autonomous municipalities and the good government boards are addressed first. This structure

2. Subcomandante Insurgente Moisés, "Regarding Pyramids and Their uses and Customary Regimes," November, 15, 2023, https://enlacezapatista.ezln.org.mx/2023/11/15/tenth-part-regarding-pyramids-and-their-uses-and-customary-regimes.

allowed the municipalities to meet others, and helped them to organize autonomously, to deploy their own systems of health and education; they learned autonomy as a practice, not as a theory. In these spaces they were able to think of themselves as peoples, to learn, "to think, to give an opinion, to propose, to discuss, to study, to analyze, and to decide for ourselves."

They also discuss the negative aspects of their formation. The EZLN points out that beyond the structure of the autonomous municipalities and the good governance boards, there were operational failures that led to "the pyramid separating the authorities from the towns." The proposals from the authorities no longer came down to the people and the opinions of the people fail to reach the authorities.

The pyramid prevented or cut off the flow of information, government was not exercised collectively or "fully," relays were not formed, and there was a tendency for the authorities to make decisions by themselves. "In other words, in summary, it was seen that the structure of how we were governed, as a pyramid, was not the way. It's not from below, it's from above." The EZLN adds that the way of governing cannot be of a military nature, and that the people "have to find their way, their way and their time," in reference to the fact that the military way of giving orders, vertical and from top to bottom, does not work.

Consequently, they decided to cut the pyramid and to turn it upside down as they realized the previous way of functioning would not allow them to properly confront the storm. This happened after multiple meetings and assemblies, where they came together and agreed on new ways of functioning that will allow them to travel on a journey of 120 years or more.

Two important issues emerge from this communiqué. The first is that structure is one thing and the way it functions is another. Structures can be used in various ways and are not as definitive as are the modes of doing things. I think this is a very important lesson for those who bet on structures without looking at how they work in practice.

Cutting off the top of the pyramid or turning it upside down is a profoundly transformative gesture. Especially when the now flattened tip was the same one they created themselves. I do not know of any other movement that has done anything similar anywhere else in the world.

The third issue is the *disappearance of symmetries,* which stems both from the decision to put an end to the autonomous municipalities and the good governance boards, as well as from the fact that the top of the pyramid was cut.

I am not saying that the EZLN has created symmetries as the axis of its policy. The point is that in a way, the autonomous municipalities that defined their territories were a counter to the municipalities of the State, just as the good governance boards were a kind of power against that of state authorities. With their disappearance and the creation of thousands of LGALs and hundreds of CGAZs, any possible symmetry/opposition with the nation-state and its structures and institutions disappears.

In this way, Zapatismo deepens its transformative character of the world, since it does not present itself as its counterpart or counterpower, but rather something completely different whose reference point is not found in the oppressor's world. Co-opting or destroying a counterpower is a real and concrete possibility, as history has taught us. But at the same time, in that very same decision, Zapatismo sowed itself into thousands of new entities that cannot be destroyed by those from above without annihilating life on the planet.

So far, revolutions and vanguards have come to replicate the system they have opposed through symmetries: revolutionary violence against reactionary violence; people's power versus bourgeois power; the workers' or proletarian state as a response to the bourgeois state, and so on in every aspect, including in economic relations. Symmetries imply that those of us who want to change the system refer to the system, shortening our horizon and the imaginary of the changes that, by acting reactively to the ruling class, continues to be dominant within our ranks.

The final issue I would like to explore is the *ethical depth* of Zapatismo. The communique, titled "Fragments," reads that they intend to "be a good seed": "We want to be the seed of a future root which we will not see, which will then be, in turn, the grass which we will also not see."[3] They propose to "bequeath life," not war or death, nor a new vision of the world for the next generation, not its miseries, its resentments, nor its pains.

This is a very strong statement made in the face of systemic political cultures. The left and the predominant world of critical thought have barely scratched the surface of something as profoundly different. Zapatismo turns systemic political cultures upside down. But neither is it the inversion of that culture, which would be a mode of symmetry, but rather they point to other modes anchored in difference.

To sow without reaping, without expecting to reap the fruits of what has been sown, is to hand over resistance and the construction of the new world to future generations without expecting anything in return, not even recognition. By renouncing the project to conquer the world to "do it again," Zapatismo distances itself "definitively and irremediably, from the current and previous political conceptions."

It is, in my view, the biggest known break with the old way of doing politics and changing the world. Sowing without expecting

---

3.   Subcomandante Insurgente Moisés, "Fragments," November 22, 2023, https://schoolsforchiapas.org/twelfth-part-fragments.

Index

AK PRESS is small, in terms of staff and resources, but we also manage to be one of the world's most productive anarchist publishing houses. We publish close to twenty books every year, and distribute thousands of other titles published by like-minded independent presses and projects from around the globe. We're entirely worker run and democratically managed. We operate without a corporate structure—no boss, no managers, no bullshit.

The **FRIENDS OF AK PRESS** program is a way you can directly contribute to the continued existence of AK Press, and ensure that we're able to keep publishing books like this one! Friends pay $25 a month directly into our publishing account ($30 for Canada, $35 for international), and receive a copy of every book AK Press publishes for the duration of their membership! Friends also receive a discount on anything they order from our website or buy at a table: 50% on AK titles, and 30% on everything else. We have a Friends of AK ebook program as well: $15 a month gets you an electronic copy of every book we publish for the duration of your membership. *You can even sponsor a very discounted membership for someone in prison.*

Email **friendsofak@akpress.org** for more info, or visit the website: **https://www.akpress.org/friends.html**.

There are always great book projects in the works—so sign up now to become a Friend of AK Press, and let the presses roll!